DIMENSIONS OF DISCIPLESHIP
A Study in the Four Gospels

Roger D. Johns

DISCIPLESHIP RESOURCES
MATERIALS FOR GROWTH IN CHRISTIAN FAITH AND LIFE

P.O. Box 189 • Nashville, TN 37202 • Phone (615) 340-7284

ISBN 0-88177-105-8

Library of Congress Card Catalog No. 91-71795

DR105B

Dedication

This study of the bibical origins of discipleship began as a series of morning Bible studies for the sessions of the Alabama-West Florida Annual Conference, May 28-31, 1989. I would like to express appreciation to my brothers and sisters of the annual conference who encouraged me to pursue this study beyond the sessions we had together.

I would also like to dedicate this volume to the following persons whose Christian witness has taught me the meaning of discipleship:

My family, including my mother, Mrs. Winnie Moseley Johns; my brother, the Rev. John Ridgeley Johns; my wife, the Rev. Louise Stowe Johns; our son, Christopher Stephen Johns; and our daughter, Catherine Michele Johns. Their love and support have allowed me to be both myself and the person God has called me to be.

The congregation of Ramer United Methodist Church for seventeen years of partnership in ministry. They were the first to read and study this manuscript. The congregation of First United Methodist Church of Marion, Alabama, was also very patient with me to hear all of this material.

The young men and women of the Alabama-West Florida Chrysalis and College Chrysalis communities. As Bishop C. W. Hancock has said, they are the future of the church and give us all hope.

Mrs. Marie Benson for her vision, inspiration, and generosity to Huntingdon College and her belief that Huntingdon may be for years to come a place where Christian discipleship is taught and learned.

Easter Sunday 1991

Contents

Preface

This study is designed to help both individuals and congregations engage in a systematic study of the four Gospels. It is specifically focused on the issue of discipleship. A dialogue is implied between the first disciples of Jesus Christ and those in his church today. The most productive setting for using this resource is a guided study involving a pastor or other informed leader and a group of serious students.

The text of this book cannot take the place of the Gospels themselves. The purpose is to offer commentary on some aspects of the biblical story. In each chapter, the Gospel in question should be read first. Then the chapter on that Gospel should be read and discussed. The book is meant to be read in sequence along with the scripture.

Questions are provided at the end of each chapter to stimulate discussion. They are only an indication of issues, however, and should not in any way limit discussion. If this book is used as a Lenten study, the six chapters can be used each week of the season between Ash Wednesday and Easter. The chapters may be spread over a longer period, however. The study may be undertaken at any time of the year, not just during the Lenten season.

When considering a subject like discipleship, it is quite clear that study alone is not enough. Discipleship must be lived. This little book can serve as an invitation to disciplined living in the example of our Lord and as a response to the call of Jesus Christ.

1
Dimensions of Discipleship

WHO ARE DISCIPLES?

This study is an invitation to discipleship. It is an invitation to discover different dimensions or aspects of discipleship as they are portrayed in the four Gospels. The basic meaning of discipleship is "to follow the discipline of a master." What, however, does it mean to follow the Master, Jesus Christ, in all of the dimensions of his discipline? This book seeks to answer this question in a straightforward and practical manner by using the dimensions through which we understand reality: height, depth, and breadth. To this is added the fourth dimension: time.

LIVING IN FOUR DIMENSIONS

Our knowledge of the physical world informs us that everything exists in three dimensions. A table can be measured according to its height, depth, and width or breadth. We shall apply this simple method to the study of the Gospels. Because we have only three dimensions with four Gospels, however, we must turn to modern physics. A fourth dimension has been added: time. According to Einstein and other contemporary thinkers, everything exists in time. This fourth dimension transforms everything. It may be seen as the transcendental dimension.

An application of these four dimensions to the study of the Gospels causes them to come alive in exciting ways. It also helps us to discover new insights into Christian discipleship.

HEIGHT

Matthew's Gospel is the Gospel of height. It calls us to follow Jesus to the height of obedience. Jesus is an authority figure for this

1

Gospel. The disciples look up to him. Jesus' sense of righteousness far surpasses that of the social and religious leaders of his day. Discipleship may be defined as obedience to his instructions and to the God whom he obeys. Following Jesus, step by step, in a winding ascent is a good description of the vocation of discipleship.

Until and unless a disciple knows whom to regard as primary authority, that disciple's life lacks direction. Obedience is the first step in discipleship. It requires looking up to the Master.

DEPTH

The second dimension of discipleship is depth, which is most clearly probed in Mark's Gospel. This Gospel stresses the responsibility of the disciple of Jesus to follow the Master in taking up his or her cross. The ultimate witness of faith is willingly and freely giving up one's life. If Matthew speaks of following Jesus to the heights of faith, Mark shows what it means to follow him into the depths.

Suffering is not something that anyone knowingly seeks, yet it is precisely suffering that Mark indicates is the change agent in life. Instead of the road to conquest, Jesus chose, as the suffering servant of God, to go the road less traveled, the road of suffering and death. The disciple is to find in the power of Jesus' powerlessness the secret witness to his ministry. Then as martyr, the disciple is to take up his or her cross and follow down the dark road into night.

BREADTH

The opposite of the dimension of breadth is narrowness. The Gospel of Luke abhors narrowness in any sense. The spiritual mentor of Dr. Luke is Paul, the missionary apostle. The refusal of many early Christians to accept Gentile converts as full citizens of the church distressed Paul greatly. Luke derived his broad view of openness and justice from Paul.

The Gospel of Luke advocates the full breadth of Jesus' message. He is the compassionate Savior, who reached out to the poor, the sick, the outcast, the wretched of the earth. Jesus anticipated Paul's missionary imperative of going to all the world with the gospel. Jesus sent out disciples to all people everywhere.

For Luke, discipleship is shallow unless and until we learn to accept those who are different and who live outside the community of faith. One of the main difficulties of any disciple is seeing in the face of a stranger the face of Christ.

TIME

Just as the dimension of time differs from the other three, so the fourth Gospel differs from the others. This Gospel moves spiritually over the boundary between time and eternity. Jesus is able to view the world from God's perspective in time, as if he is already living in God's eternity as well as in normal space and time. Seeing life in an eternal mode was hard for his disciples.

The three dimensions of discipleship discussed previously are powerful. The disciple learns from the Master how to live in terms of height, depth, and breadth. This means obedience, witness, and bearing witness. The fourth Gospel asserts, however, that this is not enough. Discipleship that does not know the differences between time and eternity cannot endure. This fourth dimension may be the most difficult to grasp. It is the spiritual realm in which discipleship finds its medium. Just as an animal lives in the air and a fish lives in the sea, so a disciple exists spiritually in eternity.

JESUS' PLAN OF DISCIPLESHIP

The four Gospels portray four different attitudes toward discipleship. Does this simply reflect different interpretations by the four sources, or are there four dimensions of Jesus' own understanding of discipleship?

Years ago, when each city had its own minor league baseball team, there were groups of boys called "knothole gangs." These boys did not have money for tickets, so they positioned themselves outside the high wooden fence that was around the ballfield. They would scurry from one hole to another so that they could get some sense of the game. The four Gospels are like this. Each offers a different view of or perspective on the same reality.

Each of the Gospels presents a unique perspective on the life and teachings of Jesus. Each has a different attitude toward discipleship, toward the major focus of Jesus' teachings, and toward almost every other major issue. This does not mean, however, that they contradict each other.

The question remains: What are Jesus' intentions concerning his followers? Does he really give us four dimensions of discipleship? I believe that he does. If we had only one Gospel, we would be rich. In reading one Gospel after another, however, our excitement grows as each dimension is added. Do you remember seeing a 3-D movie for the first time? The first view of the film was terribly out of focus. But when you put on the curious plastic glasses with one red lens and one green lens, something magic happened! The same is true of the Gospels. Dimension after dimension is added until the true parameters of the gospel of Jesus Christ and the task of his disciples are understood.

COLORFUL DISCIPLESHIP

Too often we see the life of Christian discipleship in black and white. The New Testament presents a picture of new life in Christ in living color. It affirms a polychromatic, Technicolor view of discipleship. The rainbow has become a symbol of the colorful new life of discipleship for many Christians today. This should be contrasted with the drab, colorless existence many have prescribed for followers of Jesus. Jesus was scarcely a colorless person! His followers were always finding new dimensions and new colors in his personality. One of these aspects is his pervasive humor. Many of us today need to rediscover the multidimensional nature of Christian discipleship.

PETER AS MODEL DISCIPLE

To help us understand what each dimension of discipleship means in actual life, we shall look to the discipleship of Peter as a model. Can one really find all four dimensions of discipleship in the life of one person? I believe that it is possible to find them in Peter. This is a truth, however, which does not come easily. Peter struggled and grew in each phase. He looked up to Jesus and tried to obey him. Peter strove to plumb the depths of Jesus' example, but had trouble with the idea of suffering. He wanted to accept the breadth of Jesus' compassion, but had difficulty practicing it. He reached for eternity, but kept asking what time it was.

Peter may be said to have set the parameters of discipleship: He is both the best and the worst. Being a sensitive person, he exploded with excitement when he got things right. He was mortified when he failed. Many moods and modalities of discipleship are revealed in and through his experience. Each of us can find a common experience with Peter, which is perhaps why we find him so appealing. In each of the Gospels, Peter serves as the yardstick whereby we can measure the success of Jesus in transferring his ideas to his disciples.

Ultimately it is not to Peter that we should look, however, but through his experience to the one whom he called Master. If we try to copy his experiences as a disciple, we will appear as a buffoon or the shadow of a shadow. To copy him is to become grotesque. If we are guided by his sympathetic example, we will follow not him, but his Lord.

In discipleship, it is vital, no matter whom we see as our role model, to copy not the copy, but the original. The true disciple always points beyond self to the Master. So, even as we focus on Peter, we are actually looking beyond him to the one whom he followed in obedience, in suffering, in spreading the good news, and into eternity.

Our ultimate goal then is to follow Jesus. That is what makes us his disciples. After the resurrection, the followers of Jesus continued to be referred to as his disciples. This applied both to the immediate group of the Twelve and to the larger crowd of followers who gathered around Jesus during his ministry. This wider meaning of *disciple* makes it possible for us to refer to his followers today using the same term.

The followers of Jesus are those with whom he shares and discusses his innermost thoughts, fears, desires, hopes, and prayers. It is interesting that in the Sermon on the Mount, Jesus withdrew from the crowd, went up a mountainside, and shared with his disciples (Matt. 5:1). His disciples had a special calling and responsibility to hear and to follow the Master. The same is true today. A disciple is one who studies diligently the words and deeds of Jesus, trying to get inside them and master their meaning. He or she seeks to get closer and closer to the Master.

QUESTIONS FOR STUDY AND DISCUSSION

1. To be Jesus' disciple is to follow him. Recall a time when you felt especially close to Jesus. Describe what your life as a disciple was like at that time.

2. Keeping in mind the different dimensions of discipleship as they have been explained so far (pp. 1-3), which dimension(s) is (are) most like your own experience of discipleship? Explain.

3. Which dimension(s) is (are) most like the practice of discipleship in your congregation? Explain.

4. Which dimension(s) is (are) least like your own experience? or that of your congregation?

5. The New Testament presents a picture of new life in Christ in living color (p. 4). Think of at least one dimension of discipleship, and choose a color from the spectrum to symbolize what you hope to discover in this study about that dimension. Jot down your thoughts, and share them with at least one other person.

Demention of "time"
5 - Hope to understand life
as "eternal in" the here after"
and obtain a more secure
feeling and belief of this.

2
HEIGHT
The Gospel of Matthew
and Obedience

Look to this day,
For it is life,
The very life of life.
In its brief course lie all
The realities and verities of existence.
The bliss of growth,
The spendor of action,
The glory of power—
For yesterday is but a dream.
And tomorrow is only a vision,
But today, well lived,
Makes every yesterday a dream of happiness
And every tomorrow a vision of hope.
Look well, therefore, to this day.

Sanskrit Proverb

TEACHING WITH AUTHORITY

The Gospel of Matthew was probably not the first to be written, but it is first in the hearts of most Christians. This Gospel presents discipleship at its height. In Matthew, Jesus is a person to be respected, looked up to, and seen as a role model. He is presented by Matthew as one who has authority to teach, to heal, and to lead his disciples in the right direction. A disciple in this interpretation is one who is a student of the Rabbi, the Teacher-Messiah.

In Matthew, the ministry of Jesus is an upward-winding spiral.

Jesus' disciples are literally to follow him, stepping in his footsteps, up the winding path. His authority is based on his relationship with God. It goes beyond that claimed by the scribes and Pharisees. They based their authority on the scriptures. Jesus goes further to establish his claims based on his relationship to the God who is the author of the scriptures.

Matthew's Jesus teaches his disciples "as one having authority" (7:29). This did not prevent the question, repeated often by his opposition, "By what authority are you doing these things, and who gave you this authority?" (21:23). Jesus was critical of those in authority for many reasons, most importantly, because "they do not practice what they teach" (23:3). The entire twenty-third chapter of Matthew is a critique of false authority. Jesus summed this up with one word: "Hypocrites!" The religious leaders of that day were only great pretenders. They did not live in obedience to their teachings. Jesus advised his disciples, "Do whatever they teach you and follow it; but do not do as they do" (23:3). He respected their theory, but not their practice.

In contrast to the religious leaders of his day, Jesus lived in strict obedience to what he taught. He was consistent and authentic. He was both the great teacher of righteousness and the outstanding example of the higher righteousness. Moreover, Jesus was able to confer this authority on his disciples. He passed on his authority over "unclean spirits," and he gave "instructions" for them to go out into nearby towns and villages to minister in his name (10:1, 5). Ultimately, Jesus laid claim to "all authority in heaven and on earth" and handed this same authority on to his disciples (28:18).

RADICAL OBEDIENCE

In Matthew, discipleship means taking one step at a time and following Jesus wherever he asks one to go. Often we try to run ahead to show the way. Sometimes we get so far behind that we feel lost. The first disciples felt the same way. Jesus knew, however, that they would never be able to lead the new church in the days following his death and resurrection if they were too proud to follow. The road of discipleship may seem ridiculous at times, but the Master knows where he is leading.

The biblical tradition presents many models of leadership: patriarch, judge, priest, prophet, and king. The Christian faith, which identifies Jesus as the Messiah, combines all of these models in one individual. All of these models call for obedience to the authority given by God to this individual. Leadership calls for "followship." The Messiah is one who must be followed.

The disciple is, therefore, simply one who obeys the Master. He or she must follow instructions. The word *obedience* is interesting. From its Latin roots, it contains both the idea of hearing and the idea of doing what is demanded. The disciple of Jesus is required to listen very carefully and then creatively to do what is asked.

For many of us, purchasing something that requires assembly is an adventure. We take it home, work for hours putting it together, then read the directions. Discipleship, on the other hand, can never be a do-it-yourself project. Careful attention must be given to the Master, who is to be heard and obeyed accurately and with conviction.

Radical obedience, however, is not and cannot be a wooden repetition of Jesus' words and deeds. The original disciples tried this. Often, contemporary disciples try this as well. True discipleship is creative, innovative, and inspired. For many years, discipleship in the church has been seen as an imitation of Christ. We need to come to see it as an innovation of the same spirit that guided Jesus' thoughts and actions. Obedience to the call of Jesus means responding like him to the voice of God speaking at the deepest level of our being. The disciple is one who is both addressed by God's word spoken by Jesus Christ and enabled to respond to that word by God. This means that discipleship is a vocation, a calling, which is more important than any other in our lives.

The original twelve disciples were addressed by Jesus with a call to discipleship as they went about their daily lives. When Jesus called them by the Sea of Galilee, they left their fishing and followed him. Their response was immediate and without reservation. Something deep within each of them recognized his authority over their lives, and each responded accordingly.

The disciples had no idea, of course, what they were getting into. They were called to leave not only their jobs, their families, and their homes but also all respectability in the world of their day. By following Jesus, they entrusted themselves to the care of one who constantly challenged and questioned the authority of the power structure. The mother of James and John did not understand that Jesus had no intention of conferring upon her sons the social position she wanted for them. Being an official of his "kingdom" could not be translated into any meaningful position in secular terms.

THE GREAT DISCOURSE

We can see the vertical dimension of Matthew's Gospel in many details of the relationship between Jesus and his disciples. After calling the first disciples, for example, Jesus left the crowd around him on level ground (5:1). He went up a mountainside and called the disciples to assemble around him. Then he delivered what the famous archeologist W. F. Albright has called "The Great Discourse."

This Sermon on the Mount, or "Core Curriculum" or "Instruction in Discipleship," focused the essential teachings of the Master for those who wanted to follow him. Jesus began with the so-called "Beatitudes." We could perhaps summarize them with the words, "Happy are the humble" or "Joyful are the obedient." The Beatitudes could be paraphrased: You are indeed fortunate if you

are humble,
have empathy and compassion,

are gentle,
want to live a moral life more than anything,
show forgiveness, pity, and kindness,
keep your thoughts and motives pure,
are able to reduce conflict,
suffer for doing right,
keep your cool when mean people use every trick in the book to
    try to destroy you.

These nine statements clearly cannot be written down in any law book. They cannot be systematized. They come from inside and reflect sincerity and humility at every stage. The rewards Jesus promised are gauged proportionately and appropriately to the merit and sincerity of each. They command the highest kind of internal obedience, rather than any merely external practice of rule keeping.

Jesus compared the true faith of the Beatitudes with salt of the earth (5:13), light of the world (5:14-16), leaven in the bread (13:33), and the mustard seed (13:31, 32). He also gave a comical picture of false religion. Those who try to use religion as a cosmetic simply cover up imperfections and blemishes and look grotesque. In Matthew 6, Jesus used the example of the person who came to bring his gift to church and had trumpets blowing to herald his arrival. Jesus also portrayed a person who presented a long, loud, stilted prayer in public as a wordy and ostentatious pretender. Finally, he presented the person who made a theater of fasting.

In each case, Jesus contrasted the false piety of the follower of official religiosity with the simple and higher virtue of the true disciple. In genuine faith, a real disciple gives a heartfelt gift with no strings attached. He or she prays in private and is careful to make prayer a two-way communication. No one will guess the time of abstinence and contemplation, because the true disciple remains upbeat and bears a cheerful countenance.

In the midst of this parody of the piety practiced by the phony, Jesus gave his disciples the greatest prayer in the New Testament

(6:9-13). Its petitions directed to God are meaningful only in the mouths of disciples who are willing to obey. Three of the seven petitions concern our relationships with our fellow human beings. The prayer may be paraphrased:

May we give God the respect God is due.
May we welcome God's control of everything.
May God's purposes be accomplished here and now and for all time to come.
Provide us with the basics.
Forgive us for our sins to the extent that we have forgiven those who have sinned against us.
Do not test us beyond our ability to withstand.
Keep us strong so that we won't surrender to the enemy.

This is the prayer of the serious disciple. This "no frills" prayer sums up all of the great prayers of Judaism. It presents our relationship to God in profound simplicity.

THE CONTEMPORARY DISCIPLE

Jesus' call to the height of discipleship also contains some surprises, especially for contemporary disciples. We tend to think of height as a dimension of difficulty or anxiety, but Jesus' command at the end of Matthew 6 calls us to something else—something higher yet: "Do not be anxious," Jesus commands.

How can responsible Christians not worry? What is the source of such confidence and serenity? How can Jesus say: "So do not worry about tomorrow, for tomorrow will bring worries of its own. Today's trouble is enough for today" (6:34)?

William Barclay comments on this passage,

It is not ordinary, prudent foresight, such as becomes a man, that Jesus forbids: it is *worry*. Jesus is not advocating a shiftless, thriftless, reckless, thoughtless, improvident attitude to life: he is forbidding a care-worn, worried fear, which takes all the joy out of life.[1]

Surely Jesus is speaking to us today as well as to his followers of the first century when he says, "Relax." Our time has been called "the age of anxiety." Many of us have done the exercises, listened to the relaxation tapes, practiced the biofeedback, taken the pills, and tried positive thinking. However, we still seem to be addicted to worry.

Barclay concluded his discussion of this passage with the observation that Jesus teaches us

> that worry can be defeated when we acquire the art of living one day at a time. . . . It is Jesus' advice that we should handle the demands of each day as it comes, without worrying about the unknown future and the things which may never happen.[2]

Busyness, worry, anxiety, and care are perhaps the worst enemies of serious disciples. The fear of the unknown and of those things which will never happen especially disarm us and tie us in knots.

We think of the original disciples as having lived in a time of relative simplicity compared to ours. This is not true. The first century was fraught with conflict, turmoil, wars, and rumors of war. Those early disciples, along with us, could confess with the great disciple of the fifth century, Saint Augustine:

> I have been torn between the times, the order of which I do not know, and my thoughts, even the inmost and deepest places of my soul, are mangled by various commotions until I shall flow together in Thee.[3]

What disciples of all ages seek most of all is *inner peace*. Jesus invites us freely to give over our lives to him in sincere trust. His command to relax, to stop worrying and to place all of our anxiety in his able hands is difficult for us, but it is possible.

Learning to act on this holy command is like learning to swim.

Human beings have only 10 percent buoyancy. This is sufficient, however, to allow us to float. Floating is possible only if one trusts the water. Until a person is able to relax, to trust the water, and to allow the water to buoy him or her up, it is impossible to swim. Swimming is, therefore, impossible without trust. The same is true of obedience.

When Jesus taught his disciples, "Do not worry. . . . Today's trouble is enough for today" (Matthew 6:34), he meant that they must be synchronized with themselves. He says the same to us. Søren Kierkegaard spoke of the disciple who is "present" or "contemporary" with him or herself. Kierkegaard's "contemporary disciple" is poles apart from Augustine's worn, anxious, and harried creature. This is expressed in the following statement by Kierkegaard about the timing of one's life:

> The wish is often heard in the world to be contemporary with one or another great event or great man. . . . But might it not be worth more than a wish to be contemporary with oneself? . . . Most men, in feeling, in imagination, in purpose, in resolution, in wish, in longing, in apocalyptic vision, in theatrical make-believe, are a hundred thousand miles in advance of themselves. . . . But the believer (being present) is in the highest sense contemporary with himself.[4]

By letting go of the self, the disciple is enabled to be truly contemporary with Jesus, not just in time, but also in attitude. To be synchronized with Jesus, the disciple must not be "torn between the times," but truly present to him or herself, his or her own contemporary. This means that we must be freed from the worry that takes us away from ourselves, looking back on an unresolved past or projecting us into an imagined future. In order to obey, the disciple must be present and thus able to present him or herself to the Master.

The Great Discourse of Jesus not only brings the disciple into contact with God, but also into contact with him or herself. The psychological insights here are significant. Normally we think of a disciple as one who obeys the Master in external matters. This person is one who applies the discipline of the Master. Jesus, however, emphasizes the inner life of the believer. He sees disciples as persons who are self-motivating, creative, and secure in the reason for their own actions. Unless one is "in sync," at peace, at one with one's self, there can be no discipleship.

ECONOMICS OF THE KINGDOM

The height of discipleship is not only an internal matter, however. It also has to do with the quality of our social relationships. Jesus made this clear in many of his parables. The main focus of the parables is the *management* of the life of the individual disciple and of the whole household of faith. The parables establish, therefore, a kind of "economics of discipleship," which assert the standards and values for godly living and the principles for applying them.

Some of the parables make common economic sense. Jesus asserted in the parable of the laborers: "For the laborer deserves to be paid" (Luke 10:7; see also Matt. 10:10). Other parables in Matthew, however, seem to turn common sense on its head: for example, the parable of the unforgiving servant (8:23-34), the laborers in the vineyard (20:1-16), and the parable of the talents (25:14-30). These seem to point to something beyond conventional business wisdom.

In each of these parables, there is something at stake which transcends everyday values. In the economics of the kingdom, the length of time each laborer works is irrelevant. Each person is held responsible for his or her labor, but this is also measured proportionally according to the talents and abilities given by God. Comparing one task to another is meaningless because the value system of the Master is ignored. The most important aspect of the exchange between the Master and the servant disciple is the relationship between them.

The highest values, according to Jesus, are those which lead the disciple along the way of mercy (the unforgiving servant), compassion (the laborer in the vineyard), and responsibility (the parable of the talents). The calmness and serenity of Jesus' command, "Do not be anxious," is balanced here by the maturity and altruism of a consciousness not only of what must be done, but of how it is to be undertaken. In *Murder in the Cathederal,* T. S. Eliot has Thomas à Beckett utter these valuable words: "The last temptation is the greatest treason: To do the right deed for the wrong reason."

For Christian disciples, the task of discipleship has always been to transform theory into practice. Every act of discipleship requires a look upward to the Master and a look outward to the brother or sister in need. Jesus summarizes this key "economic" principle of discipleship: "Truly I tell you, just as you did it to one of the least of these who are members of my family, you did it to me" (Matthew 25:40).

DISCIPLESHIP IN A NEW KEY

According to Matthew, Jesus' first disciples certainly had a high calling. Furthermore, we know that after Jesus' resurrection, these original disciples became the strong, self-reliant agents of the Master who literally began the church. They were able to match serenity and calmness with toughness, maturity, and faithfulness. They practiced the radical obedience Jesus had taught them. Before all of this took place, however, the disciples had to taste the emptiness of anxiety, defeat, and disobedience.

The high road of discipleship led inevitably to the cross. This was true in the disciples' experience of following Jesus and in their own individual walks as well. On the last night of his life, Jesus was with them before he was taken by his enemies. He predicted, "You will all become deserters because of me this night" (26:31).

This began to come true immediately when they all went to sleep in the garden while he prayed. When Jesus was taken prisoner, they all abandoned him. They stood helplessly by as the events of the trial and the crucifixion proceeded. They stood at the foot of the cross, where they tasted their bitterest tears. They knew neither how to act, nor how to react. They did not realize that Jesus was still leading them and that soon they would once again know how to follow him.

As in a surrealist painting, the footprints of the Master led up to the edge of reality and everything stopped. On Easter, however, the disciples found that inexplicably the footprints continued on the other side. Even more amazing, they were to continue to follow the Master. They were disciples of a risen Lord! His leadership had not stopped; it had been transformed. All that had been invested was not lost but had come to have infinitely greater value. Discipleship had not lost its focus; it had succeeded beyond anyone's dreams. As the disciples listened to the risen Lord, the dimension of height came to have its full significance. Jesus instructed them,

> All authority in heaven and on earth has been given to me. Go therefore and make disciples of all nations, baptizing them in the name of the Father and of the Son and of the Holy Spirit, and teaching them to obey everything that I have commanded you. And remember, I am with you always, to the end of the age (28:18-20).

Dietrich Bonhoeffer summarized the meaning of discipleship for Matthew's Gospel with the statement, "Only those who obey can believe."[5] This idea is never more strongly emphasized than in this passage. Even in this mode, Jesus was still exhorting his disciples to obey. He is still Master and they are still disciples. The height of discipleship truly is obedience.

The first disciples had to climb many mountains and take many winding trails to follow Jesus: in the Sermon on the Mount, at the Transfiguration, at the Crucifixion, and with the Great Commission. At times they stumbled and fell in their attempts to follow. Nevertheless, they continually found him before them, ever beckoning to them, urging them onward and upward. As they continued to look up to him, they learned to obey and came to a faith which has changed the world.

ROCK OR MARSHMALLOW?

How did Peter react to the height of discipleship as demanded of him in Matthew's Gospel? How did this "model" disciple, this "everyman," grow in his faith? Peter is prominent throughout the Gospel of Matthew. At times Jesus indicated that Peter had heard him better than the others. Jesus seemed to confer authority on Peter and to depend on him. At other times, however, it seemed that Peter was the least responsible of the disciples and the least able or willing to follow Jesus anywhere. Seldom was Peter neutral, this either/or disciple. Jesus referred to him as "rock," but often he seemed to be marshmallow.

In perhaps the greatest test of Peter's role as disciple, Jesus asked the apostles at Caesarea Philippi who they thought Jesus was (16:15). Peter jumped ahead in his thoughts and said with intuitive and spiritual insight, "You are the Christ!" Standing there at the foot of Mount Hermon, the largest "rock" in the country, Jesus punned on Simon Peter's name and called him Peter, the Rock. He then commended Peter with the strongest words applied to any disciple:

You are Peter, and on this rock I will build my church, and the gates of Hades will not prevail against it. I will give you the keys of the kingdom of heaven, and whatever you bind on earth will be bound in heaven, and whatever you loose on earth will be loosed in heaven (16:18-19).

Following Peter's affirmation, Jesus gazed intensely southward, all the way down to Jerusalem in his mind's eye. Buoyed up by

Peter's startling insight, Jesus set his face toward Jerusalem and resolved to go there to suffer and to die.

When Jesus spoke of his intention to suffer to change the situation of humanity, however, Peter did not at first follow. He tried to change Jesus. Peter wanted to become the teacher and have Jesus as his pupil. The response of Jesus was as stinging as it once had been laudatory. He said simply and emphatically, "Get behind me, Satan!" (16:23).

Peter was a model disciple when he looked up to Jesus. Peter was also a model of failed discipleship, however, when he lost his vertical focus. At times he showed maturity of faith and displayed qualities of leadership and greatness. At other times, he was petty and childish. Through all these experiences, Jesus never gave up on him. Jesus could tolerate the flashes of brilliance, on the one hand, and the disappointing foolishness and desertion, on the other. Because of his love for Peter and because he understood what Peter would become, Jesus gave him the benefit of his enduring trust and support.

Nathaniel Hawthorne told the story of "The Great Stone Face." In it, the protagonist, a man named Ernest, lived in a valley that was presided over by a great rock which featured a formation in which many saw a human face bearing the noblest of characteristics. Over the years a number of heroes came back to the valley of their birth, hoping that they bore the likeness of the stone face. None came close, however. During this time, Ernest lived out his life in humble obedience to his faith, always looking up to the noble face in the rock. After many years, it was noticed that Ernest's face resembled the stone face. He was visited by a poet, who asserted that "the being and the character of Ernest were a nobler strain than he had ever written." As he gazed at the noble face of Ernest, he exclaimed: "Behold! Behold! Ernest is himself the likeness of the Great Stone Face!"[6] Soon there was affirmation throughout the valley that Ernest was indeed the very personification of the face.

Peter gazed up at the face of the Master. He looked up to the

Master so long and so well that he became the solid disciple the Lord always knew he would be. At times, it is true, he looked down and lost his focus and his perspective. He was always able, however, to regain his composure when he looked up again. Gradually, almost imperceptibly, he came to resemble not only the person the Master wanted him to be, but the Master himself.

QUESTIONS FOR STUDY AND DISCUSSION

1. Jesus' sense of authority, and his standard of obedience, went well beyond that of the religious leaders of his day (pp. 9-10). Are there ways in which following Jesus today also requires going beyond the standards of the religious establishment? Explain.

2. Compare the provisions of the Sermon on the Mount in Matthew 5 with the provisions of the Ten Commandments in Deuteronomy 5. Notice what is said positively in the former and negatively in the latter ("Thou shalt not . . . "). What does this say to you about the nature of discipleship and obedience in Matthew? *Positive attitude .*

3. Kierkegaard said that contemporary disciples are better off than the first disciples of Jesus. The original disciples could easily have missed the point of Jesus' authority. We know today who Jesus is. Do you agree that we are better off? Why or why not? *Bible + other text Jesus belief in religion . m*

4. The way of discipleship in Matthew might seem contradictory to some because it calls both for a higher standard of righteousness (inward and outward) and for a lower level of anxiety, stress, and worry. How would you explain this apparent contradiction to someone else? How do you deal with this in your own walk as a disciple? *Live by the golden rule, your best and realize you have strived to do*

5. In seeking to follow Jesus on the high road of obedience, the first disciples remembered Jesus' parables about how to treat each other—to be merciful, not to compare or judge each other according to their own standards of "fairness," and to remember that each person is accountable to God for his or her use of individual gifts or talents. The disciples also came to experience failure, forgiveness, and renewed vision. What does all of this tell you about our interdependence with each other in seeking and maintaining the high road of obedience?

We must be tolerant and non-judgemental and also responsible for our own actions.

3
DEPTH
The Gospel of Mark and Witness

> Let nothing disturb you,
> Let nothing frighten you,
> All things are passing;
> GOD NEVER CHANGES.
> Patient endurance
> attains all things;
> One who possesses God
> is wanting in nothing;
> GOD ALONE SUFFICES.
> *Prayer of St. Teresa*

THE SUFFERING SERVANT

If the Gospel of Matthew presents a faith by which to live, the Gospel of Mark is written to those who are forced to face death for their faith. Mark explores the difficult dimension of the depth of human suffering. Height and depth bracket discipleship and give us our first chance to contrast perspectives. They also set out the boundaries of the relationship between God and persons as mediated by Jesus Christ.

Matthew's Gospel reaches to the heavens. Mark's Gospel plumbs the depths. We see evidence of the Christian holocaust in a Christian equivalent of Psalm 130: "Out of the depths I cry to you, O Lord!" The Gospel of Mark leads inevitably to the cross. In it, Jesus speaks, as it were, from his cross to those who are called to suffer for their faith. The saints and martyrs of all ages are honored in this little Gospel. Mark moves from baptism to crucifixion in the shortest space of any of the Gospels. His work has been called a passion story with a long introduction.

The word *martyr* comes from a Greek root which means "witness." The ultimate witness is the willingness to give over one's life for what one believes. This can mean intentionally acting in such a way so as to call down punishment upon oneself because of one's faith. It can also be interpreted indirectly, as in Paul's words, when someone offers him or herself as a "living sacrifice" (Romans 12:1). Every disciple of Jesus Christ should realize that faith has been transmitted through the willing sacrifice, direct and indirect, of thousands of saints and martyrs. Suffering for one's faith leaves a witness which is impossible to overestimate.

It could be said that the entire New Testament can be seen as a magnificent footnote to the so-called "servant of God" passages of Isaiah 40-55. Isaiah 53 speaks of the "suffering servant." This concept had a more direct influence on Jesus' understanding of his identity than any other in the scriptures. He clearly understood the Messiah as one who suffers to change things. Others in his day wanted a king who would throw out the Romans, a saintly priest who would purify religious practice and piety, or an apocalyptic figure who would bring the judgment of the end time. All of these images are reflected in the New Testament, but the unexpected martyr figure of Isaiah most clearly corresponds to Jesus' self-understanding.

Likewise, the little letters attributed to Peter stress the significance of Jesus' suffering. Peter is generally seen as the source for John Mark's Gospel and for the two letters that bear his name. If this is indeed correct, there is a clear link between these works. That linkage is the redemptive power of human suffering.

First Peter especially emphasizes the importance of suffering for the disciple:

For to this you have been called, because Christ also suffered for you, leaving you an example, so that you should follow in his steps. . . . He himself bore our sins in his body on the cross, so that, free from sins, we might live for righteousness; by his wounds you have been healed (1 Peter 2:21, 24).

The last phrase is quoted directly from Isaiah 53:5. The Christian is "called" to suffer as Jesus did (1 Peter 2:21). One who suffers for his or her faith will be blessed (3:14). One who suffers as Christ did "has finished with sin" (4:1).

THE FAITH OF THE MARTYRS

The apocalyptic works in the Bible present the dire situation in which people of faith are forced to risk the ultimate sacrifice for their faith. The word *apocalypse* means both "hidden" and "revealed." The books of Daniel and Revelation are the only completely apocalyptic books in the Bible. Many other such works were written in the periods immediately before and during the time that the New Testament was written. They reflect a time when it was necessary to write or to speak in a code that would be understood by people of faith, but would not be comprehensible to the enemy.

One of the clearest explanations of this dual nature of apocalyptic language is Jesus' response to the disciples' questions after he told them the first parable. He said to them,

To you has been given the secret of the kingdom of God, but for those outside, everything comes in parables; in order that
> "they may indeed look, but not perceive,
> and may indeed listen, but not understand;
> so that they may not turn again
> and be forgiven" (Mark 4:11-12).

The adaptation here of the quote from Isaiah 6:9-10 fits perfectly the assumption in Mark that Jesus purposefully spoke on two levels.

Apocalyptic thought is often confused with prophecy. An easy indicator of the difference between the two is the attitude of each toward human history. Prophecy sees the future going on through the historical process. Apocalyptic thought finds the situation so bad that human history must end in order for there to be any future at all. God will no longer work through history. A new post-historical period will begin in which God will rule directly in God's kingdom. In Mark's Gospel, Jesus' opening proclamation strikes a distinctly apocalyptic note: "The time is fulfilled, and the kingdom of God has come near; repent, and believe in the good news" (1:15).

For Jesus in Mark, the time is short, and the disciples must consider the gravity of their calling. Discipleship means witnessing the end of history, as we know it, with all the pain that this represents. It also means welcoming the in-breaking of God's kingdom and God's ultimate rule, which will follow the historical period. This gives added significance to Jesus' invitation to gain one's life by losing it. Death must be faced squarely. It cannot be escaped. The only solace is the fact that the time before the end will be blessedly short. If the horrors of the end time were prolonged, no one could stand it. The sign of "the desolating sacrilege" of the destruction and desecration of Jerusalem and its Temple will be an indicator (13:14). This will portend the end of human history and the final triumph of God with the coming kingdom.

The Gospel of Mark, the epistles of Peter, and the books of Revelation and Hebrews show the effects of the Christian holocaust, which began in the dramatic period between the deaths of Peter and Paul in A.D. 64 and the destruction of Jerusalem in A.D. 70. It is difficult to think of two more devastating blows to the early Christian community than the loss of its apostolic leadership and the destruction of the mother church in Jerusalem. How could the church survive such events? We now know that what seemed to them to be an end was a beginning. The suffering of the saints and martyrs made this possible. All of this, however, was not evident from their vantage point.

CASTING OUT DEMONS

The Gospel of Mark comes second in our Bibles. Most scholars consider it, however, to have been the first written. This opinion is based in part on nothing more sophisticated than the fact that it is the shortest. Logically things seem to move from simple to complex. It also contains less mortar between the building blocks of tradition. Matthew and Luke have a certain stylistic graciousness and charm, which are totally lacking in Mark. This gives Mark's Gospel an angular, abrupt, tough quality. Jesus gave simple answers to complex questions. For example, in Mark the reason the opponents do not understand Jesus is not so much their refusal to try (as in Matthew 13:13-15), but the fact that God does not want them to understand (4:10-12). Jesus is pictured in Mark as dynamic, moving about somewhat frenetically, and constantly casting out demons. We might call him the "Dynamic Healer" in this Gospel.

In Mark's Gospel, there is a war going on. This is part of the struggle of the end time. Healing, performing nature miracles, and resuscitating are part of Jesus' struggle with the powers of evil. They swirl about constantly trying to defeat him. The healing work of Jesus is not treated in the same manner as in the Gospel of Luke, the physician. Jesus does not so much perform miracles that defy the laws of nature, as he labors on a deeper level with God to heal, to strengthen, and to bind up what is broken.

If we speak of "casting out demons," it seems to make the Gospel curiously obsolete and unusable. On the other hand, if the depth dimension is stressed along with the urgency of the end time (anticipating imminent disaster), then perhaps the modern reader can get beyond this stumbling block. John Mark may not be using the word *demon* solely as a part of the medical vocabulary of his day. He is perhaps using this terminology to indicate the battle in which Jesus was engaged.

In apocalyptic literature, a characteristic feature is the battle of good and evil for mastery in the world. It may well be Mark's intention to show that Jesus is constantly engaging the enemy and winning. Healing, nature miracles, and resuscitations help bring in the new age.

The Gospel of Mark contains more accounts of healings than the other three. Furthermore, more emphasis is laid on Jesus' role as Dynamic Healer. The healings carry out the inaugural theme of 1:15 in that the forgiveness of sins is responsible for healing. When the opponents of Jesus chided him for associating with sinners, he responded, "Those who are well have no need of a physician, but those who are sick; I have come to call not the righteous but sinners" (2:17).

In the same chapter, Jesus said to a paralyzed man, "Son, your sins are forgiven." The opponents were incensed and commented: "Why does this fellow speak in this way? It is blasphemy! Who can forgive sins but God alone?" (2:5-7). Jesus' followers, however, were "amazed and glorified God, saying 'We have never seen anything like this!'" (2:12). This was more than a physical healing. It was a metaphysical event. Strengthening the faith of the individual and of the disciples was as important as healing a person's diseased or malformed body. Jesus did not separate the two.

In all of this, however, a question can be meaningfully raised: If Jesus is the great healer in Mark and goes about relieving pain, conquering evil, and stilling storms, how then can suffering be the main focus of the Gospel? How can Mark be the Gospel of depth, of following Jesus through the valley of suffering and death?

If we are true to Mark, we will not move too quickly or easily to a resolution of this apparent contradiction. For Mark, the happy news of healing and victory in the first part of his account was clearly interrupted by increasing signs and warnings of Jesus' suffering. As the Gospel proceeds, one feels the rising fear of the disciples as they try to deal with what they sense, but do not understand. In this context, Jesus does not abandon the conflict with evil. He calls his disciples to join with him in a new way of engaging the battle. The resolution of the apparent contradiction is ultimately seen only as they follow him on the way of redemptive suffering.

The task of discipleship is to follow Jesus in the conflict between good and evil, even to suffer for the sake of bringing an end to violence, fear, and further suffering. For those who have no faith in themselves, in the Master, or in God, the depth dimension of faith is frightening, unfathomable, and inscrutable.

Mark's Gospel is a drama in depth. It shows how the faith of the original disciples was tested, and it tests the faith of contemporary followers of Jesus as well. It is a kind of morality play in which everything moves on one of two different levels, depending upon the faith of the witness.

THE SON OF GOD

In Mark's Gospel, disciples must live by faith and not by knowledge, as we normally understand it. They must rely on God who gives them understanding. Apocalyptic literature does not seek to contradict human reason. It does, however, assert the idea that understanding is not possible without a key, a code, an answer to the mystery of human life, which is hidden. Only the person of faith, to whom God's answer to the human condition is revealed, can see in this poor man Jesus, who suffers for his faith, God's will for the world.

In Mark's Gospel, the disciple is enabled to perceive in faith the true nature of God's truth. In reality, God wants the faithful to be well, to be healthy, to be whole, to live, and to be happy. This purpose of God is often interrupted, however, by the forces of evil. Apocalypticism is strongly concerned with the problem of why it is that God's faithful suffer. The suffering here, even unto death, is certainly "real," in this-worldly terms. The disciple, however, must see this from God's perspective. The pain of life now is only temporary, and not eternal. The promise is given that God will wipe away every tear from the eyes of the faithful.

The climax of Mark's Gospel may well be the confession of the centurion, "Truly this man was God's Son!" (15:39). Jesus' suffering and death paradoxically constituted the healing event which potentially opened the hidden truth of his identity to everyone, even the Roman centurion. The ability to see God's power in the powerlessness of a man tortured and killed by Roman cruelty was the ultimate test. Not even the disciples of Jesus saw it yet, but this centurion did. This was a clear sign that things had changed. God's new age had begun as that which was hidden had become plain.

In Mark's Gospel, Jesus predicted his death at least three times (8:31-33; 9:30-31; 10:32-34). Each of these instances may be called "the gospel in a nutshell" because everything in Mark is ultimately connected with Jesus' suffering and death. Jesus told his disciples, as they were coming down from the mountain of the Transfiguration, that they were "to tell no one about what they had seen, until after the Son of Man had risen from the dead" (9:9). The death of God's Son was the crucial element for understanding his identity and purpose. It was also the event that would bring God's kingdom to its fulfillment. The disciples were not to speak openly until after Jesus' death; the event would loose their tongues.

Jesus not only referred to his own death, he also explicitly announced to the disciples what the result of their discipleship would be. They would not be spared their own crosses:

> If any want to become my followers, let them deny themselves and take up their cross and follow me. For those who want to save their life will lose it, and those who lose their life for my sake, and for the sake of the gospel, will save it. . . . Those who are ashamed of me and of my words in this adulterous and sinful generation, of them the Son of Man will also be ashamed when he comes in the glory of his Father with the holy angels (8:34-38).

There was unblinking realism in Jesus' appraisal of what it would take to change the human situation. If persons fear for their lives, they are not fit for discipleship. Jesus was not foolhardy, and he did not call upon his disciples to be foolish either, but he knew that the cost of discipleship was great.

Jesus had learned the lesson of Isaiah, which was that redemptive suffering could change the world. Perhaps this was the most important thing he taught his disciples. He combined this notion with the apocalyptic insight that things were so bad that only God's invervention would alter the course of the world. These two convictions determined the level upon which Jesus worked and to which he called the disciples to witness. Death is a necessary ingredient. This fact is not necessarily morbid; it is simply the inevitable conclusion. A commitment is required which will literally take the disciple beyond life in the historical sphere. This is not tragic, as Jesus did not measure life simply in historical terms. The presentation of his challenge to live out of history understandably caused fear and consternation among his first disciples, as it does today. Jesus' goal, however, was to bring his disciples from fear to faith.

FROM FEAR TO FAITH

Quite possibly, the last words of the Gospel of Mark are "they said nothing to anyone, for they were afraid" (16:8*b*). Some of the most dependable ancient texts end here. Others go on to give a brief account of the resurrection and end with 16:20. Whether "fear" is, in effect, the last word or not, it is the final enemy. The church community in the time of the composition of Mark knew that the disciples had overcome their fears. To leave them quaking in their sandals would have been an offensive anticlimax. By adding the resurrection account, the church accented the fact that fear had been conquered for them and could be conquered for those facing death at the hands of the Romans in the Christian holocaust.

Lamar Williamson, Jr. commented on the many failures of the disciples of Jesus and the willingness of the Master to calm their fears, to forgive them and to give them another chance:

> The disciples in Mark reflect the enthusiasms, misunderstandings, and failures characteristic of the Marcan community and of each succeeding generation of Christians. . . . When Jesus calls disciples to follow him, he calls us. When Jesus rebukes obtuse disciples, relatives and friends, we stand convicted. When, even after the disciples have contradicted, denied and abandoned him, Jesus promises to go before them into Galilee and reveal himself to them there, we are confronted by his forgiveness and offered the hope of another chance to follow him.[7]

Williamson goes on to say that if discipleship means comparing ourselves to Jesus, "disciples always fail." Indeed, accepting the role of disciple of Jesus Christ means accepting failure. In the eyes of a success-oriented society, Jesus fails, and his disciples fail with him. In this sense, we are called to accept failure. This is what it means to bear one's cross, to accept one's suffering, to offer one's body "as a living sacrifice, holy and acceptable to God" (Rom. 12:1).

It is no wonder that the disciples were filled with fear! Following Jesus is a fearful thing. The Gospel of Mark delivered the bad news about suffering and death with little or no sugar coating. It cannot be said that Jesus ever deceived his disciples by hiding the reality of his destiny or that of his followers.

Mark also presented the good news of God's forgiveness for our fear and failure, however. The victory accomplished through Jesus' suffering and death aroused perhaps the most uncanny fear in the disciples. Dare one believe such a thing? The reality of this event was not only Jesus' victory over the powers of evil, sin, and death, but also God's ultimate victory over the vicissitudes of human history through his Son, Jesus Christ.

Søren Kierkegaard descibed three stages of life:[8] (1) The "aesthetic stage" is characterized by the desire for immediate gratification; "I want it, and I want it now!" (2) The "ethical stage" is based on obedience to laws and knows some self-denial for a lofty goal or cause. (3) The "religious stage" embraces suffering and sacrifice for the supreme goal, "the pearl of greatest price." Kierkegaard said that suffering is "the distinguishing mark of religious action." We suffer because we have been "committed to relative ends." A true disciple of Jesus Christ is involved in "dying away from immediacy." The disciple must practice painful renunciation. The individual who wants to become a disciple of Jesus Christ must say no to self-gratification, must go beyond "the law of the scribes and Pharisees," and ultimately must deny self completely. This necessarily means that the disciple has to experience the bitterness of suffering, not simply in terms of defeat or failure (as in Matthew's Gospel), but as a way of sharing in the suffering of Christ on behalf of others.

Mark's Gospel plumbs the depths of discipleship. Like the apocalyptic book of the Old Testament, Daniel, it takes the disciple into the lion's den and into the fiery furnace. It presents a theology of the cross, which also means an apocalyptic view of the gospel. Jesus' suffering and death make the suffering and death of the disciple necessary. It is also true, however, that Jesus' victory over sin, evil, and death make the victory of the disciple possible.

The message of Mark is simply this: The person who would follow Jesus Christ as disciple will of necessity face a cross. The logic of this is unfortunately unconditional and inevitable. Jesus paid a high price for the freedom of the disciple. The disciple must pay a high price as well. There is no such thing as "cheap grace," according to Bonhoeffer: "Cheap grace is grace without discipleship, grace without the cross, grace without Jesus Christ, living and incarnate."[9]

Kierkegaard, Bonhoeffer, and a host of others echo Mark's theme: Do not be surprised that suffering comes because of the commitment of faith. Suffering is the inevitable price of discipleship, but it is worth it. This value judgment is not something that anyone else can understand vicariously. Just as there is no such thing as secondhand faith, there is also no such thing as borrowed discipleship. Each person must take up his or her cross. This is a part of the challenge of discipleship.

Suffering calls forth more suffering. Yet, suffering is the only way that suffering can be overcome. The suffering of the cross brought to Jesus' lips the bitter words of the psalmist: "My God, my God, why have you forsaken me?" (Psalm 22:1; Mark 15:34). A theology of the cross is a God-forsaken theology. The God who forsakes the Son also validates everything the beloved Son has said and done, however. The centurion saw this paradox in the power of powerlessness (15:39). Paul knew it when, in weakness, he found God's strength (2 Cor. 12:8-10).

God is often closest when God appears to be absent. The lines below were found written on a wall in the cellar of a building in which Jews were hidden during World War II. The unknown author asserts:

I believe in the sun, even when it is not shining.
I believe in love, even when feeling it not.
I believe in God, even when God is silent.

The suffering, that seems to cut us off from God, and even brings us to the point of God-forsakenness, has precisely the opposite effect. This suffering for the sake of faith not only joins us to Christ, but leads us to "communion with God," as Bonhoeffer aptly puts it:

Hence while it is still true that suffering means being cut off from God, yet within the fellowship of Christ's suffering, suffering is overcome by suffering, and becomes the way to communion with God.[10]

Mark's Gospel offers no detour around suffering and no means of avoiding the cross. It places the depth dimension squarely before us. Much about the mystery of suffering remains hidden. This is the nature of the apocalypse. Yet much is revealed also. The drapes are drawn, an obscure hand pulls back the corner, ever so slightly, and a transcendent face is almost seen. This revelation is only a hint, but that is enough of a witness for faith. We stand before a mystery, perhaps the greatest mystery of all: the mystery of life and death, and the meaning of both. These come together in the words, "For those who want to save their life will lose it, and those who lose their life for my sake, and for the sake of the gospel, will save it" (Mark 8:35).

Even though Mark 13 speaks of the end of time, it does not attempt to provide an exact time frame. The destruction of Jerusalem and the desecration of the Temple were signs of the end. Nevertheless, the exact time and place were not clear. The disciple is admonished to "Watch!" The end can really come at any time, or it can be delayed. Apocalypticists like Mark are not necessarily "wrong" because of their assertions concerning the nearness of the end of history. What is important in their work is that they take their time with ultimacy.

For those who are going through suffering, pain, and guilt, this sense of time holds the promise of being on the way to deliverance and healing from addiction, enslavement, and illness. The disciple reaches out in faith. Jesus responds with his healing power, and the demons are cast out. A disciple is precisely one who knows the healing power of Jesus in one's own life. Jesus enables this person to live out of history and into eternity, as a citizen of God's in-breaking kingdom. In this sense, history has ended and the new age has begun in the life of the disciple.

When betrayal, inhumanity, insults, and destruction become the order of the day, the disciple must find meaning from another source, outside of the present order which has become unbearable. Thank God that the day of suffering has been shortened, "for the sake of the elect" (13:20). The disciple is focused and calm, unlike those who scurry about, lost and frightened. The disciple knows what time it is and becomes a source of salvation for others. The believer redeems the time. The disciple sees behind appearances to what God is doing in the world, in, through, and beyond the historical process. In Barclay's words, true disciples "live in the shadow of eternity." [11]

THE COWARDLY LION?

In Frank Baum's *The Wizard of Oz,* one of the most imaginative characters is the cowardly lion. He has a noble heart, but fear seems always to keep him from being who he wants to be. Fear is a form of faithfulness that crippled Peter and still cripples many disciples of Jesus Christ.

This fear in Peter is ironic because Peter is the disciple who has come to be known as the source of Mark's Gospel. In the accounts of Peter's association with Jesus, however, he was the disciple who consistently tried to keep Jesus from suffering. He tried to talk Jesus out of going to Jerusalem. He brought a sword to the garden to fight those who wanted to inflict pain and injury on his Lord. He even cut off a man's ear. This same Peter, however, was crucified in the persecutions of Nero. According to tradition, when Peter learned of his fate, he asked that the cross be inverted because he was unworthy to die in the same manner as his Master. There is no rejection of suffering here. One cannot hear any hint of cowardice in Peter's voice. What has happened to Peter in the time between his discussions with Jesus about suffering and the time of his own death?

Peter took courage from Jesus and became the disciple he was called to be. The word *courage* contains the Latin root for "heart." The true disciple takes "heart" from his Lord. Peter, the cowardly lion, talked a good show, but lacked heart. The Gospel of Mark is a tough person's Gospel. It is the gospel according to Peter. His true toughness is not in his physical strength, however, but in his spiritual power. It took him a long time to learn this. When Peter responded to Jesus' challenge with the words, "Look, we have left everything and followed you" (10:28), Jesus responded with what amounts to, "So what?" He was not impressed with what Peter had sacrificed. Jesus saw how much Peter was holding back. When Peter said, like a tired athlete, that he had given all he had, Jesus, like a good coach, demanded more.

Perhaps the most painful minute of Peter's life was early in the morning after Jesus had been siezed by his enemies. While Jesus was being interrogated by the authorities, Peter waited in the courtyard. When he was recognized by a servant of the high priest, he denied three times that he had anything to do with Jesus. Then a rooster crowed and Peter remembered how Jesus had predicted, "Before the cock crows twice, you will deny me three times" (14:72). His cowardice led to desertion and denial. He had once forbade Jesus to suffer, but now Peter, in a sense, had become one of those who tormented Jesus. Peter's unwillingness to suffer himself had caused the suffering of his Master and of others. All of his brave words tasted like ashes in his mouth.

On Easter morning, three women went to finish treating the body of Jesus, preparing it for burial. A "young man" dressed in white told them about the empty tomb and sent them back to the disciples with the message, "But go, tell his disciples and Peter that he is going ahead of you to Galilee; there you will see him, just as he told you" (16:7). Peter was singled out in this command. Jesus was giving him a new chance! This time Peter was to hold nothing back. He was healed of his fear and free to give his witness.

Peter no longer suffered from the secret affliction of cowardice. His faith and the Master's healing touch made him whole. In *The Wizard of Oz,* the cowardly lion lacked courage. In the course of the story, however, he received the encouragement necessary for him to grow. The same is true of Peter.

The church has come to use the lion as the symbol for the Gospel of Mark. The lion here is really Peter. His courage has become proverbial. He is no longer the cowardly lion. He has become a true disciple of the Lion of Judah (Genesis 49:9; Proverbs 30:30; Revelation 5:5).

QUESTIONS FOR STUDY AND DISCUSSION

1. How do people in your congregation and/or community view suffering? Which of Kierkegaard's three stages—aesthetic, ethical, religious (p. 34)—seems to be most prominent?

2. What preconceptions today make it difficult to think of Jesus both as one who heals us and as one who suffers and calls upon us to suffer?

3. How does Mark's interpretation of redemptive suffering change, confirm, or expand your appreciation for the depth of discipleship?

4. What does redemptive suffering accomplish? Can you give examples from your own experience of those whose sacrifice has made a difference in your life? in your congregation? in your community? in the world?

5. In view of the depth of discipleship in Mark's Gospel, name some specific ways that you and your congregation can follow Jesus in the way of redemptive suffering.

1. Ethical stage = obedience to laws and some self denial.

4
BREADTH
The Gospel of Luke and
Bearing Witness

The face of God is the face of justice.
God is in every person;
Justice is in every person.
Justice does not change,
only the nature of justice changes.
Attributed to King Urakagina of Lagash, 2600 B.C.

JESUS AS THE UNIVERSAL SAVIOR

We have made considerable progress with both the vertical and the depth dimensions of discipleship. Now we shall add the horizontal dimension. Otherwise, we are still only in two dimensions. For width or breadth, we now turn to the Gospel of Luke. In relation to Luke, breadth means the spread of the gospel to all the world. It also signifies a passion for fairness, justice, and equality.

Luke certainly combined these qualities. He spoke out of a church community which had accepted him, a Gentile, into full membership. Luke was introduced to Christianity by Paul. He then set out to become a devout disciple of Jesus Christ. Like Paul, he saw the church as a redemptive community in which it did not matter whether one was rich or poor, Jew or Greek, male or female, slave or free (Galatians 3:28). One came into this community as one came in from the cold and warmed oneself before going back out into the wider world. This reciprocal movement still forms the necessary ebb and flow that keep the church alive.

Luke was one of the greatest apologists the church has ever seen.

41

He was able to present the gospel in a way which the cultivated, educated, and wealthy people of his day would understand and find credible. In both his Gospel and in his unique history of the early church, the Book of the Acts of the Apostles, he displayed what can best be termed, the "wideness in God's mercy." He made the exciting discovery that the missionary imperative in Paul's work already existed in the ministry of Jesus. Paul did not invent it—he simply continued it. This is the key to Luke's perspective and his Gospel. God's message of salvation is universal and has become, in Simeon of Jerusalem's words, "a light for revelation to the Gentiles" (2:32).

Both the Gospel of Luke and the Book of Acts were dedicated to someone designated only as "Theophilus," whose name means, "a lover of God." He was a person of wealth and power to whom Luke wrote in order to present his unique version of the good news. Paradoxically, however, this good news may have tested Theophilus in some ways, as we shall see. The mission and message of both Jesus and Paul stressed the broadness and openness of God's love. The message of salvation could not be restricted to those whom the popular theology asserted were worthy because of their position, wealth, and influence. On the contrary, Dr. Luke saw Jesus as a universal Savior, who was a healer of souls and a minister to the outcast.

Just as the writer of Isaiah 40-55 was the first to see the world-historical importance of Judaism, so Luke was the first to see the significance of Jesus as the Savior of the whole world, from pole to pole, and from creation to consummation. As the judge of all human history, Jesus assumed a critical position for Luke in God's scheme of things, not just for Jews, but for all peoples. This dimension of breadth is comprehensive in space and time. The theme of universal judgment is accompanied, however, by universal justice and mercy. The world situation in Luke's day was terribly unfair. The rich and powerful, like Theophilus, were assured the best the Roman Empire could furnish. The numberless poor, however, had nothing. Jesus as universal judge would right these wrongs and herald a day of universal justice.

LOVE AND JUSTICE

In Luke's Gospel, Jesus was very much involved in healing, but in a way different from the healing accounts in Mark. This probably reflects the fact, attested by tradition, that Luke was a practicing physician. Rather than concentrating on the struggle between good and evil, as Mark had done, Luke saw Jesus as the Compassionate Healer. Jesus reached out in love to the poor, and the outcast, those who were physically or mentally ill, and those who were persecuted because of their race, age, sex, or religion.

His ministry of healing was also a ministry of saving. Forgiveness of sins was a part of the healing process. Reaching out in love, forgiveness of sins, and healing were all part of the same process. Jesus commented concerning the woman who bathed his feet with her tears and dried them with her hair: "Therefore, I tell you, her sins, which were many, have been forgiven; hence she has shown great love. But the one to whom little is forgiven, loves little" (7:47).

Belief and salvation are connected. Jesus encountered a woman who had touched him and was cured of an ailment that had lasted twelve years. To her he said, "Daughter, your faith has made you well; go in peace" (8:48). Then Jesus spoke with a man named Jairus about his daughter. Soon thereafter, they were interrupted by a messenger announcing her death. Nevertheless, Jesus responded, "Do not fear. Only believe, and she will be saved" (8:50). He then went home with Jairus and raised her from the dead.

In these miracles, we see a causal link between faith, forgiveness, love, healing, and salvation. This linkage is different from what we saw in Mark, however. In Mark, faith allows one to understand when suffering interrupts healing. In Luke, faith is the source of healing.

Faith and healing work perhaps in a circle or spiral, rather than in a straight line, but they are connected. Luke the physician emphasized this connection. He knew that ultimately healing is salvation, and salvation is healing.

The Jesus of Luke's Gospel is not only motivated by redemptive and healing compassion, he is also one who has a consuming passion for justice. He is partial to the poor. Matthew stresses "the poor in spirit"; Luke focuses on the poor and the lost. Luke 15 features the parables of the lost: the lost sheep, the lost coin, and the lost son. Chapter 16 stresses wealth versus poverty: the parable of the dishonest manager, the law and the kingdom of God, and the rich man and Lazarus. In the parable of the widow and the unjust judge, Jesus comments: "And will not God grant justice to his chosen ones who cry to him day and night? Will he delay long in helping them? I tell you, he will quickly grant justice to them. And yet, when the Son of Man comes, will he find faith on the earth?" (18:7-8). Here justice and faith are closely related.

In the story of Jesus' trial and execution, Luke focuses more on the question of justice than the other Gospel writers. Perhaps Luke knew more about how the judicial system should work than the others. According to Luke 23, Pontius Pilate and Herod Antipas clearly understood that there was no basis for the charges against Jesus. Both found him innocent and even struck up a tenuous friendship based on their association and agreement on this issue. Pilate tried to go against public opinion, but the mob forced his hand. Instead of releasing Jesus, according to the practice of honoring the holiday by freeing a felon, he released Barrabas, the charges against whom included, starting "an insurrection that had taken place in the city, and for murder" (23:19). The baseless charge against Jesus was "perverting the people" (23:14). Pardoning the man guilty of the more serious crime made the situation all the more ridiculous. Pilate washed his hands of the matter! The same Roman centurion who affirmed Jesus as God's Son in Mark, commented in Luke's version, "Certainly this man was innocent" (23:47; Mark 15:39).

Love and justice meet in the person and work of Jesus. In Luke 6, his version of the Beatitudes contrasts the rich and the poor: "Blessed are you who are poor . . . " and "Woe to you who are rich . . . " (6:20-26). In this passage, the concerns of love and justice were clearly articulated.

Wealth and possessions are not in themselves wrong. The problem is that they draw one away from love and justice. The rich ruler who came to Jesus is clearly a case in point. After affirming him and his lifestyle, Jesus added, "There is still one thing lacking. Sell all that you own and distribute the money to the poor, and you will have treasure in heaven; then come, follow me" (18:22). The man walked away grieving (Matt. 19:22; Mark 10:22). He was vulnerable and unable to comply because his possessions really owned him. He was not open to others; he had to tend to his own concerns. He could not become a disciple.

The German theologian, Jürgen Moltmann, tells the story of his experience as a prisoner of war following World War II. He was a sixteen-year-old who was forced to become a soldier for a matter of months. For this he was captured and taken for several years to a camp in Scotland where he was forced to perform manual labor. The cold damp weather was bad for his health.

One winter he had a terrible cold and no handkerchief for his nose. He was forced to use his coat sleeve for the excessive nasal discharge. The coarse material became stiff and abrasive. It felt like sandpaper on his raw nose. He looked up from his work to see a group of local peasant women and children standing with the military guards observing him and the other prisoners. One of the women looked directly at him for some time. She then spoke with one of the guards and handed him something. The guard walked over and gave Moltmann an old white rag. At first, he only stared at the nondescript piece of cloth in his hand, failing to understand what had happened. Then, suddenly, it dawned on him what she had done.

This was easily one of the most significant gifts he had ever received. It helped to change his life. The act did not cure his cold, nor did it free him from incarceration. The direct expression of love and justice came from one who knew what it meant to be without the essentials of life. Moltmann expresses doubt that a rich person would have thought to give him something for his predicament. The old woman had just the right thing for his need: not a starchy new handkerchief, but a soft, worn rag. This was an act of grace, and she gave it to a hated German prisoner! She lived her discipleship. She became Christ for this young man and helped heal his loneliness, despair, and suffering.

RESPONSIBLE DISCIPLESHIP

Chapter 10 is the turning point in Luke's Gospel. Up to this point, the disciples have listened, observed, and stored up all of Jesus' instructions. At this point, Jesus challenges them to go out and to bear witness. This witness is their testimony of faith. A disciple is one who expresses the faith in his or her own way.

In the prologue to this Gospel, Luke speaks of "eyewitnesses," "servants of the word," and those who have written "an orderly account of the events that have been fulfilled among us" (1:1-4). These three represent, respectively, the first disciples, the apostles, and the scholars, such as Luke, who presented their testimonies in their writings. Each disciple of Jesus reaches a point of ripeness or maturity in which he or she must give expression to the faith. To fail to do so is to fail as a disciple.

Chapter 9 of Luke parallels the first two Gospels with the sending out of the twelve. Chapter 10 is unique with the sending of the seventy. This clearly anticipated the general missionary effort of sending disciples to all seventy nations of the then-known world.

The seventy were sent out to proclaim good news to the poor, the outcast, and the ill. They were also to practice love and justice with deeds of goodness and compassion, following the example of Jesus Christ. The orthodox cities of Chorazin, Bethsaida, and Capernaum were to be avoided, however, because of their previous refusal to receive the gospel. It was not among the rich, the powerful, and the doctrinaire that the gospel would be heard and practiced, but among the poor, the ignorant, the rejected, and the pagan.

The seventy were sent out two by two, barefoot, and without purse or provision. There is a vagueness of time and place which perhaps indicates that this misson applies to Luke's own time as well. Actually the sending of the seventy applies to any time the church reaches out to the world. The living Christ commissions his disciples, and they go out. They are promised that he will follow them and then meet them on the way to celebrate their victories in his name.

In Chapter 10, Luke is preoccupied with methodology. How did Jesus send his disciples to bear witness in the world? What was his practical methodology for mission? Luke's scholarly approach here probably worked backward from his intimate knowledge of Paul's missionary message and method to its grounding in the teachings of Jesus. The wonderful results of Luke's scholarship indicate that the two fit well together. Paul was a man of action, but his theory was deeply rooted in the thought of Jesus. Jesus was not only a preacher, teacher, miracle worker, spiritualist, and mystic, but he was also one who sent his disciples out on a mission. Luke arrived at the truth that the mission of the church was not conceived in Antioch by Paul and his associates. It was already an integral part of Jesus' own teachings. The methodology for going out to win converts and to form new churches did not begin with Paul. It was already present in the ministry and in the instructions of Jesus to his disciples.

In Luke, the sending of the seventy comes just after Jesus ended his ministry in the north. Following the Transfiguration, Jesus "set his face to go to Jerusalem" (9:51). The disciples were sent ahead as

Jesus began his own epic journey. In this sequence, the sending assumes its full importance. Jesus' mission and the disciples' missionary activity complement each other. The true role of each disciple only really begins with being commissioned into Jesus' missionary service.

Like a young eagle, the neophyte disciple must test his or her wings. The Holy Spirit was the wind beneath the wings of the fledgling. Until and unless he or she left the nest, however, and was tested in mission, there could be no true discipleship.

Disciples were sent out as "lambs into the midst of wolves" (v. 3). They were to greet each town or village with a hearty, "Shalom!" If they were greeted in return and accepted, they were to do deeds of love and justice there. If not, they were to move on. In either case, they were to proclaim the nearness of the kingdom of God. Their actions showed the same boldness characteristic of the disciples in the Book of Acts. At the conclusion of the mission, the seventy returned to Jesus, joyfully saying, "Lord, in your name even the demons submit to us!" (10:17).

ACCOUNTABLE DISCIPLESHIP

David Lowes Watson speaks of four "dynamics of discipleship":

(1) the *call* to discipleship,
(2) the *form*,
(3) the *power*, and
(4) the *method* of discipleship.[12]

These four steps effectively outline Chapter 10 of Luke's Gospel. Watson calls them components of "accountable discipleship." He is speaking of the early Methodists, but this describes the disciples of Jesus as well. Watson comments,

The early Methodists worked out their salvation in the reality of worldly living, empowered through the means of grace afforded by the time-honored disciplines of the church. They did this by exercising a mutual accountability for their discipleship in the context of Christian fellowship.[13]

For Luke, discipleship means being mutually accountable to Jesus, to other disciples, and to those who are served.

According to Watson, the method of the early Methodists was integral to the success of their mission. Like Jesus' "method," this included a well-defined mission, a discipline to follow, and a way to be held accountable. Methodology is crucial for successful discipleship. Through it, followers of Jesus become "disciplined disciples."

When the mission of the seventy was completed, Jesus' joy could scarcely be contained. Luke commented that he "rejoiced in the Holy Spirit" (10:21). Jesus did not hide his exuberance in the following verses: "Blessed are the eyes that see what you see! For I tell you that many prophets and kings desired to see what you see, but did not see it, and to hear what you hear, but did not hear it" (10:23-24). In very few instances in all of the Gospels does Jesus express so strongly his pleasure with his disciples.

By holding the disciples accountable, Jesus entered into a partnership with them. This same partnership has always been the basis of successful discipleship. In it, the disciple is held responsible, on the one hand, and given the support and encouragement needed, on the other. In terms of Jesus' care and training of disciples, Chapter 10 is the climax of Luke's Gospel.

THE ROLE OF THE HOLY SPIRIT

For Luke, a disciple is like an Old Testament prophet or a New Testament apostle. Each was called by God and enabled by the Holy Spirit. Without these two prerequisites, discipleship would be only a human action. One must be empowered to be a disciple of Jesus Christ.

The Holy Spirit plays a much greater role in the third and fourth

Gospels than in the first two. The Spirit is an active force for Luke, working through the inspired prophets of old, who anticipated the Messiah, and through the disciples, who are empowered to serve him. Jesus spoke of the Holy Spirit's instruction to the disciples concerning what they were to say and do (12:12). The mission, launched by Jesus in Chapter 10, will be carried on in the age following his death and resurrection. The force driving the mission is the Holy Spirit. A disciple of Jesus Christ is one who is called by Jesus and empowered by the Holy Spirit to do God's work in the world.

A disciple is one whose life has been "turned around," given direction, accountability, and responsibility, and sent on a mission for God. Luke mentions the conversion of Paul at least three times in Acts. Paul himself had referred to it at least once in his work: "God, who had set me apart before I was born and called me through his grace, was pleased to reveal his Son to me, so that I might proclaim him among the Gentiles . . . " (Galatians 1:15-16). Luke applied this concept of conversion in both of his works. A disciple of Jesus Christ is called by God, "turned around," and directed specifically toward a mission or goal. The mission, the goal, and the guidance system are motivated and directed by the Holy Spirit.

The popular understanding of conversion today is often perverted by at least two misunderstandings: On the one hand, conversion is defined by heavy-handed manipulation. This has been called "snapping," or breaking the will of the believer and rendering the person powerless with regard to the sect or cult. On the other hand, conversion is often seen as a vacuous, smiling, squeaky clean transformation of the believer.

The role of the Holy Spirit in conversion in both Luke and Acts is categorically opposed to these distortions. A disciple of Jesus Christ is one who has been transformed, neither into someone else, nor into an ideal form of humanity, but from inauthentic to authentic existence. This person is no longer alienated or estranged from essential being, but is able to live fully the life for which God has created him or her.

THE WALK TO EMMAUS

Luke 24:13-35 contains a unique account of the risen Lord's appearance to two disciples on their way back from Jerusalem to their village of Emmaus, a seven-mile journey. One man is named Cleopas; the other person's name is not given. They are discussing what happened to Jesus and how his followers felt about it. They were numbed by the events which they had recently witnessed. The risen Jesus joined them and entered into the discussion.

Jesus interrupted them saying, "Oh, how foolish you are, and how slow of heart to believe all that the prophets have declared! Was it not necessary that the Messiah should suffer these things and then enter into his glory?" (vv. 25-26). His rebuke seems almost cruel and rather abrupt. Yet, the rebuke was needed. These disciples of Jesus had seen their faith almost destroyed by the crucifixion. They referred to the resurrection, but without conviction or feeling. They reported what they had seen, but they did not bear witness or give testimony. They got the facts right and were able to report to this stranger with accuracy, but without conviction. The reason he chided them is their lack of faith. Their witness died stillborn. They could not bear witness. It is not enough simply to transport or to sustain the message. It must come to life again in the telling!

The full Emmaus Road account is given only in Luke's Gospel. The story is perhaps the entire Gospel in a nutshell. In it the main theme of Luke's theology is stressed. The faith of the disciple is dead unless it comes to renewed expression, growing out of the person's own experience. If it is presented in the lifeless manner of these two witnesses on their way to Emmaus, there will be no church! As advertising executives know, nothing is so appealing as a personal testimony. Conversely, nothing is phonier than a false or lifeless testimonial.

The Emmaus Road story continued as Jesus backed up what he had told the two persons with lessons from the scriptures. When they reached the village, they invited Jesus to stay the night. During the evening meal, he was finally disclosed to them in the breaking of bread. "When he was at the table with them, he took bread, blessed and broke it, and gave it to them. Then their eyes were opened, and they recognized him; and he vanished from their sight" (vv. 30-31).

Jesus' teaching from the scripture was followed by the Eucharist, or Holy Communion. The two disciples were stunned by what had happened. After time to reflect on these events, they commented, "Were not our hearts burning within us while he was talking to us on the road, while he was opening the scriptures to us?" (v. 32).

Upon returning to Jerusalem, the two repeated the process of observation, reflection, and accurate reporting of what they had seen. This time, however, they were not able to contain themselves. Although certainly tired from their long walk and exhausted by the emotional ordeal, they nevertheless bore witness to what they had seen and heard. The difference between their earlier report to Jesus and their testimonial to the Jerusalem community could not be more pronounced. It is the difference between simply going through the motions and enthusiastically presenting one's testimony concerning the risen Lord.

No account in Luke's Gospel is directed so specifically to the theme of discipleship as the Walk to Emmaus. From this story we learn about the measure of effectiveness of discipleship. The person doing the evaluation is none less than Jesus himself. The lesson for disciples can be summarized as follows: The disciple is to walk with Jesus. Yet, more than that, the disciple is to observe the life and teachings of Jesus as revealed in the Old and New Testaments. By reflecting on all of this, the disciple develops a personal perspective.

Finally, the disciple is to share the story with others from his or her own unique personal point of view.

In the encounter with Jesus on the Emmaus Road, the two disciples shared a complete worship experience with the risen Lord: In his interpretation of the scriptures, in his breaking of bread, and in his compassionate counseling and prophetic ministry to them. They literally came to faith in a way that had never occurred in their lives before. Their willing and eager response to this conversion experience was to go and share this faith with others. Their vibrant enthusiasm in turn brought others to faith, and then still others, in a chain reaction that moves from person to person, from place to place, from generation to generation, across all boundaries and obstacles.

CHANGING VALUES

When a person becomes a disciple of Jesus Christ, that person comes to value her or himself in a new way. This value system does not see a person in terms of what that person possesses, but in terms of what Jesus Christ has done for him or her. For the disciple to confess that Jesus Christ is Savior and Lord of life is to acknowledge, "I have been rescued from a life of meaninglessness."

Jesus had great appeal to those who were poor, who were ill, who were outcasts, and who were considered wretches. Among the rich, the powerful, and those with excellent health, he was not so successful. Their sense of values and deceptive feeling of security was fool's gold. They believed they were important and that their lives were going somewhere. This deception was (and is) hard to overcome. Jesus referred to this: "How hard it is for those who have wealth to enter the kingdom of God! Indeed, it is easier for a camel to go through the eye of a needle than for someone who is rich to enter the kingdom of God" (18:24-25).

The rich do not know that they need to be saved; the poor do.

There is, therefore, no advantage to being rich. Indeed, there is great disadvantage. In terms of kingdom values, riches are a terrible liability.

Jesus saves the disciple from narrowness, self-centeredness, and preoccupation with personal concerns, and turns that person toward the needs of others. This is the basis for ministry: sensitivity to the needs of others. The rich and powerful do not realize that others exist and have needs. They have been taught to presume that others exist only to serve them.

Luke's Gospel presents the original "liberation theology," without any basis in Marxism. This theology of salvation does not cater to the whims of the rich and powerful. It also does not look at the world through rose-colored glasses, promising a utopia to the poor and the disadvantaged. Like Jesus, when he overturned the tables of the moneychangers in the temple, this view of liberation overturns the values of present society. A person cannot become a disciple unless and until he or she is saved from these false values.

The Savior is also the Redeemer. Jesus paid the price for those who had no resources against evil, sin, and death. Our value system is changed when we know the costly price he paid. Essentially, both the rich and the poor have been controlled by the same false sense of values. The only difference is that the one has seemingly benefited from it and the other has seemed to suffer from it. In light of what God has done in the events of the life, death, resurrection, and ascension of Jesus Christ, both rich and poor are freed from a system which ultimately cannot win for either because it has falsely pitted them against each other. Jesus has become "the hinge of history," in the words of theologian Carl Michalson. Our lives pivot on the Christ event from meaninglessness to meaning, from being lost to being saved, from damnation to salvation.

THE TWO-FACED DISCIPLE?

Where do we find our friend Peter in all of this? Confused as usual. Paul called him two-faced because he pretended to accept the Gentiles as full members of the church until the conservatives from Jerusalem arrived: Then "he drew back and kept himself separated for fear of the circumcision faction" (Galatians 2:12). The early church faced a serious threat of splits developing between the differing communities based on narrowness, pettiness, discrimination, and shortsightedness. After having passed the tests of obedience and suffering, will Peter fail on the issue of discrimination?

Peter had a powerful vision at Joppa in which his faith was opened to the Gentiles (Acts 10). He also provided a powerful witness for Paul's ministry to the Gentiles at the Jerusalem Council (Acts 15). These events happened after the experiences he had with Jesus during his three years of ministry. Tolerance, openness, and a broad approach to discipleship evidently did not come easily to Peter. As an observant Jew, he had been taught to separate himself from others, especially Gentiles. How could the Master want him and the others to associate with people who were not ritually "clean"?

Peter first met Jesus in Capernaum. After teaching in the synagogue, Jesus went to visit Peter, whose mother-in-law he healed (4:38). Peter's next encounter with Jesus took place on the Sea of Galilee (5:3). Jesus got into Peter's boat and told him where and how to fish. The catch was so great that the other boat belonging to Peter had to come over and help. Peter was deeply moved and said to Jesus, "Go away from me, Lord, for I am a sinful man!" Jesus responded reassuringly, but also prophetically: "Do not be afraid; from now on you will be catching people" (5:8-10). Peter had no idea how many nets he would cast out in the future and into how many different seas.

It is difficult to measure the effect of Jesus' ministry on his disciples until after his death and resurrection. They began as hard and opinionated persons. They had difficulty giving up age-old prejudices and ingrown bigotry. For many in Jesus' day, these were a part of organized religion. The softening and nurturing effect of Jesus' ministry of love and compassion, justice and mercy had its transforming power in the lives of the first disciples. In his last speech to the disciples before his ascension, Jesus commanded them:

> Thus it is written, that the Messiah is to suffer and to rise from the dead on the third day, and that repentance and forgiveness of sins is to be proclaimed in his name to all nations, beginning from Jerusalem. You are witnesses of these things. And see, I am sending upon you what my Father promised; so stay here in the city until you have been clothed with power from on high (24:46-49).

Ultimately Peter and the other disciples did go to all nations. Peter overcame his former reticence about the Gentiles. When the Holy Spirit came upon the disciples at Pentecost, it was Peter who proclaimed the gospel to an international forum consisting of persons from at least a dozen countries (Acts 2:1-36). Peter applied the lessons learned from years of sailing the Sea of Galilee. He set his sails and turned into the wind with his face toward the distant shore. He knew the breadth of his mission and its comprehensive scope. Going to the world with the gospel did not allow him involvement in disputes over issues between Jews and Gentiles. From his experiences of vacillating between petty narrowness and the true openness of the gospel, Peter became the disciple with one face.

Finally, one would like to know the words exchanged between Peter and Paul in the Roman jail cell in which they were held just before they were taken out to be killed. Surely they bore witness to Jesus Christ. There must have been a harmony of spirit and a sharing of experiences between them which gave ample testimony to the breadth of discipleship.

QUESTIONS FOR STUDY AND DISCUSSION

1. According to Luke, Jesus sent his disciples on a mission to the whole world. Do you think the church today still sees the world as a mission field? Why or why not?

2. Some people question whether religion is of any earthly value. How might Luke's account of the link between faith and healing and faith and justice help in responding to this question?

3. What is your understanding of conversion? How does this compare with Luke's description of a process, empowered by the Holy Spirit, which frees you to be all that you can be in witness and service to the whole world?

4. Have you ever had an experience like Moltmann's where someone reached across cultural, social, or other group boundaries to show compassion to you? Describe your own experience, or describe what you think Moltmann must have felt.

5. Luke's account of the breadth of discipleship led him to reflect considerably on the "method" of discipleship—on matters such as going out two by two and returning to make a report, being accountable. Why do you think these kinds of considerations are particularly important when we seek to take the breadth of discipleship seriously?

6. In what ways can the church today live out the breadth of discipleship as described by Luke? How do (or can) you and your congregation do this?

5
TIME
The Gospel of John and Spiritual Growth

HIGH FLIGHT

Oh, I have slipped the surly bonds of earth
    And danced the skies on laughter-silvered
        wings
Sunward I've climbed, and joined the tumbling
        mirth
    Of sun-split clouds—and done a hundred
        things
You have not dreamed of—wheeled and soared
        and swung
    High in the sunlit silence. Hov'ring there,
I've chased the shouting wind along, and flung
    My eager craft through footless halls of air.

Up, up the long, delirious, burning blue
    I've topped the wind-swept heights with easy
        grace
Where never lark, or even eagle flew—
    And, while with silent lifting mind I've trod
The high untrespassed sanctity of space,
    Put out my hand and touched the face of
        God.[14]

THE FOURTH DIMENSION

With the three dimensions described in the first three Gospels, our study of reality in space is complete. To know anything, the height, depth, and breadth must be measured. We have done this. The fourth Gospel, however, presents us with another dimension. Contemporary physics, building upon the work of Einstein and other modern theorists, tells us that time is a dimension. The first three dimensions develop the boundaries of space. The fourth dimension deals with duration.

In a recent issue of *National Geographic,* an article titled "The Enigma of Time" detailed the development of the modern concept of time. In 1905, Albert Einstein blasted Sir Isaac Newton's concept of time as an absolute. Because of Einstein's theories of relativity, "time was first seen as a dimension—like height and width—giving meaning to events and the order in which they occur. Time, quite literally, was something that keeps everything from happening at once."[15]

Two years after Einstein's monumental discovery of time as a dimension, the mathematician Hermann Minkowski popularized Einstein's theory with "a new geometry that adds time to the three dimensions of space. This four-coordinate system, space-time, caught on as an efficient way to simplify Einstein's formulas."[16]

The shift of interest here from space to time parallels our interest. In shifting from the three dimensions studied previously, we now take up a dimension that separates events in terms of duration. We shall also, however, look at the spiritual aspects of the life and thought of Jesus in John's Gospel. How does Jesus' spirituality touch different modes of time, and still connect the whole of time simultaneously?

John's Gospel is clearly different from the other three. Almost everything is unique. It is spiritual, sacramental, and mystical. In this Gospel a tension exists between time and eternity. Barclay expresses this in the following: "John did not see the events of Jesus' life simply as events in time; he saw them as windows looking into eternity, and he pressed towards the spiritual meaning of the events and the words of Jesus' life in a way that the other three gospels did not attempt."[17]

One of the most difficult aspects of Einstein's concept of time is the theory of relativity. He asserted that time is not absolute, but is relative to one's position and to the speed at which one is moving. John's Gospel represents a kind of spiritual relativity. Jesus presented to his disciples a concept of existence which is not bound by time. He challenged them to see life from God's perspective in eternity.

John's Gospel is both the simplest and the most complex. In the other three, one observes each event from one perspective. In John, we must learn to see everything *multidimensionally*. This is the difference between looking down into the muddy Red River and into a clear Colorado mountain stream. In John, every sign, every act has an inexhaustible number of layers of reality. This is the difference between perceptions in time and in eternity.

Contemporary ideas of time are often bound by the limitations of space. We cannot conceive of anything without thinking of it in terms of our concepts of time and space. These are only concepts, however, and limit our perception. God is not limited by our conception of time or space. God exists in another order of things. We can never really begin to see things as they are until we are able to see with God's eyes in a way that transcends the limitations of time and space.

In John's Gospel, Jesus is a time traveler who exists simultaneously in a past which extends back before the creation of the world, in a present pregnant with the wisdom of all time, and in a future which reaches into eternity and infinity. It is difficult to grasp this fullness in a person who expresses the most profound aspects of humanity. Jesus is both fully God and fully human without these being in contradiction. He lives fully in time, without being time-bound.

THE WORD COMING INTO THE WORLD

John does not begin with an account of the birth of a child in a manger. This Gospel does not tell the story of the development of character in a young person. It does not trace Jesus' life until the time of the beginning of his ministry. It begins with a metaphysical prologue, which is simultaneously a meditation on creation and on wisdom: "In the beginning was the word [*Logos*] . . . " (1:1).

In order to express Jesus' identity as the embodiment of the divine creative principle by which God created all things, the writer of this Gospel used perhaps the most profound word in the language of both Greek theology and philosophy: *Logos*. By using this word, John sought to say that Jesus is the very wisdom, reason, and mind of God. The writer of Proverbs asserted long ago: "The Lord by wisdom founded the earth . . . " (3:19). Barclay comments that John raised this combination of creation and wisdom to assert to both Jew and Greek alike "that in Jesus Christ this creating, illuminating, controlling, sustaining mind of God had come to earth."[18]

This is the principle of incarnation, one of the most awesome and wonderful concepts in the entire New Testament. The divine creative principle (*Logos*) by which God has done all things has come into the world (1:14). "The world" here should be understood temporally, however, and not just spatially. "The world" is a time of darkness and alienation. In opposition to "the world," Jesus represents "light" and "life," two of the great themes of this Gospel. The world is a place of temporality, mortality, and decay.

Jesus continually points away from the world to God's eternal kingdom of uninterrupted duration, immortality and renewal. Every sign and symbol in John's Gospel indicates this perspective. One of the most familiar passages in John also illustrates this point: "For God so loved the world that he gave his only Son, so that everyone who believes in him may not perish but may have eternal life" (3:16). This passage cannot be fully comprehended if "world" is understood simply as a physical place. The physical world is God's good creation. It does not need redeeming as such. What is in need of redemption is the quality of human life in time. This is the "world" that God loved.

Human life is expressed in terms of a time span. This duration must have its place. Indeed, human life is bound to the time-space continuum. It is also, however, only through time that place or space can be overcome. Eternal life is an understanding of the removal of the limitations of the place of human life through extension of its duration. The Gospel of John has done for the spiritual comprehension of time what Einstein did for the physical understanding of time. The world in which we live has been transformed and transcended by an act of new creation through the coming into the world of the divine creative principle in Jesus Christ.

ETERNAL LIFE

In John's Gospel, eternal life does not begin with death. It starts when someone begins living in eternity, when one is "born from above." Jesus said to Nicodemus, "Very truly, I tell you, no one can see the kingdom of God without being born from above" (3:3). Nicodemus, of course, understood Jesus initially in the literal sense of actually being "born again" from his mother's womb. This reminds us of the statement in John's prologue, "But to all who received him, who believed in his name, he gave power to become children of God, who were born, not of blood or of the will of the flesh or of the will of man, but of God" (1:12-13).

Physical birth brings us into the world, into time. Spiritual birth takes us out of the world, into eternity. Barclay comments on the Greek word for eternal life:

This word has to do, not so much with duration of life, for life which went on forever would not necessarily be a boon. Its main meaning is *quality* of life. There is only one person to whom the word *aiōnis* [eternity] can properly be applied, and that is God. Eternal life is, therefore, nothing other than the life of God. To possess it, to enter into it, is to experience here and now something of the splendour, and the majesty, and the joy, and the peace, and the holiness which are characteristic of the life of God.[19]

To have eternal life is truly to live in God. This was what Jesus practiced and also what he sought to impart to his disciples. In his great prayer in Chapter 17, Jesus stated as his divine mission, "to give eternal life to all whom [God has] given him" (v. 2).

Eternal life is living through time and the world in touch with eternity. Jesus commented, "Whoever believes in the Son has eternal life" (3:36). This is a good definition of what it means for John to be a disciple of Jesus. In an especially poignant scene, many of his disciples had left Jesus because of the scandal of his words. Peter responded to Jesus' question, "Do you also wish to go away?" with the words, "Lord, to whom can we go? You have the words of eternal life" (6:67-68). A disciple is one then who learns from Jesus what it means to live in eternity.

THE LOVE COMMANDMENT

It is ironic that in a Gospel filled with eucharistic allusions (e.g., "bread of life," "the true vine"), there is no account of the Last Supper. Instead, in John 13, on the eve of the Passover, Jesus performed the task of a servant and washed the disciples' feet. In a dry and dusty land, with domestic animals running free, and open sewers, feet got rather dirty. One was expected to remove one's shoes and to walk on mats in a Jewish home. The task of footwashing was, therefore, more than just a common courtesy. It was an act of personal hygiene and a social necessity. It was usually performed by servants.

On this evening, however, the disciples had ignored the common practice. They had simply taken their places at the table, reclining with their dirty feet extended away from the table. After taking off his outer garment, Jesus began to wash their feet. He started at one end of the table, and moved systematically from one disciple to another. He finally reached Peter, who at first refused Jesus' attempt to wash his feet. There was a commotion at the table that resulted in the surfacing of various opposing emotions. Jesus then explained to the group that friendship with him required this kind of vulnerable and trusting service. The lesson of footwashing is expressed in Jesus' great love mandate: "I give you a new commandment, that you love one another. Just as I have loved you, you also should love one another" (13:34-35). One who lives from above, and is in touch with the eternal, is willing to serve others out of reciprocal love for God and for fellow human beings. This kind of love is not possible except as it comes from God and is given back to God in service to other people. This kind of love endures.

The word *agapē* means self-sacrificial love. It is used two hundred times in the New Testament, about seventy of which are in John's writings and an equal number in Paul's epistles. This theme is central to each of the five New Testament books attributed to John and is particularly well stated in the first of the three brief epistles that bear his name: "God is love, and those who abide in love abide in God, and God abides in them. . . . We love because he first loved us. . . . The commandment we have from him is this: those who love God must love their brothers and sisters also" (1 John 4:16-21). Here "love" is not merely an emotion. It means finding the central guiding force of one's being in God and in the other person. Here love represents the highest and purest form of altruism, as displayed in the life and death of Jesus Christ.

THE SPIRITUAL PRESENCE

Chapters 13-17 of John's Gospel have been called the "Intimate Discourses" of Jesus. In this section Jesus speaks to his disciples indoors, as opposed to the public ministry which took place primarily outside. His words are directed to his closest followers and not to everybody. Some of his comments seem to indicate a future discussion, but they certainly describe this entire section as well: "I have said these things to you in figures of speech. The hour is coming when I will no longer speak to you in figures, but will tell you plainly of the Father" (16:25). The atmosphere of this section is intensely spiritual. It reminds one of the ambience of a Rembrandt painting or the ethereal quality of a Bach oratorio. Its directness, earnestness, and intensity are unparalleled in the rest of the Gospel of John.

In what might be called "Jesus' Last Will and Testament," he shared his most important teachings with those who were to carry on his ministry after his death. He taught them that the reality of his life (eternal life) would continue with them even after his death. In Chapter 13, he began this crucial part of his ministry with the washing of the disciples' feet. He then consoled his disciples concerning his approaching death with the words, "Do not let your hearts be troubled" (14:1). Then, according to John, Jesus introduced the promise of the Holy Spirit.

In his account of Jesus' teaching about the Holy Spirit, John uses the Greek word *parakletos*. This word was familiar in ancient courts of law. It meant "advocate, counsel for the defense, one who intercedes." The word is used only once in the New Testament outside the Intimate Discourses. There, in 1 John, it refers to Jesus' role as the eternal advocate of believers in heaven: "We have an advocate [*parakletos*] with the Father, Jesus Christ the righteous; and he is the atoning sacrifice for our sins, and not for ours only but also for the sins of the whole world" (2:1-2).

In the Gospel of John, however, Jesus applies this title to the role of the Holy Spirit. Jesus will die, but when he departs this world, he will not leave his friends without counsel. Indeed, it is to the advantage of believers that Jesus goes and the new counselor or advocate comes (16:7). This advocate, the Holy Spirit, is "the Spirit of truth," who will speak on the disciple's behalf, will teach him or her, will provide guidance and support, and ultimately will convince and convict the ruler of this world (14:15-17; 15:26; 16:12-15).

Like any good defense counsel, the Advocate not only upholds the party accused and presents the case on that person's behalf, but also is able skillfully to attack the false accuser. Jesus has done this on a scale limited by his humanity during his ministry. So will the Holy Spirit, the Advocate and Counselor, do the same on a much grander scale after Jesus' death and resurrection. According to John, all of this began when Jesus pronounced the words, "Receive the Holy Spirit" (20:22) as his disciples gathered together following the resurrection.

Thus, for John, the life that Jesus gives to the disciples is not limited by Jesus' physical presence. Jesus is able to continue to be with the disciples through the power of the Holy Spirit, even beyond death. This is shown in the unique way in which Jesus functions as a priest in John 17.

John 17 is probably the dramatic climax to the entire Gospel. It has been called "the High Priestly Prayer." As we read through this prayer, we get a sense that Jesus was intimately present with his disciples in the last minutes before he turned himself over to his enemies. Jesus' words also indicate, however, that he was metaphysically present with God in the heavenly kingdom as he spoke, looking directly to God: "I glorified you on earth by finishing the work that you gave me to do. So now, Father, glorify me in your own presence with the glory that I had in your presence before the world existed" (vv. 4-5).

In addition, we need to remember that this account of Jesus' prayer was written years later, around A.D. 110. The way the prayer is framed indicates an awareness that Jesus' presence has continued to be witnessed sacramentally in the writer's own church. Thus, Jesus' prayer already echoes the words that the priests would later use to celebrate Jesus' continuing presence in the sacrament of the Lord's Supper: "And this is eternal life, that they may know you, the only true God, and Jesus Christ whom you have sent" (17:3).

The high priestly prayer indicates three different modes of Jesus' presence with his disciples. These three modes describe the spiritual, mystical, and sacramental levels upon which everything occurs in the fourth Gospel. Moreover, these all occur simultaneously. It is interesting that the church has come virtually to identify the incarnational Christology of John with the concept of the real presence of Christ in the church. These two come together in the sacraments of the church.

In John, Jesus is a time traveler. His ability to travel in time enables him to be the Redeemer of humanity, as well as God's agent of creation. He literally saves the time of our lives. The event of salvation is real, but it is also only describable in spiritual, mystical, and sacramental terms. The worldly time-space continuum has no vocabulary to describe what happens in being born "from above." Because the life of Jesus transcends time as we know it and makes time relative to his purposes, he is able to be present with his disciples, with God, and with the contemporary believer.

THE TIME OF DISCIPLESHIP

One of the most difficult problems for the disciple of Jesus Christ is knowing what time it is. The great philosopher of time, St. Augustine, described clearly the three phases of time as we perceive it in the *Confessions:*

Perhaps it might be said rightly that there are three times: a time present of things past; a time present of things present; and a time present of things future. . . . The time present of things past is memory; the time present of things present is direct experience; the time present of things future is expectation.[20]

The very act of writing the Gospel is an exercise in time for John. The discovery of each level of time is an act of faith dependent upon the work of the Holy Spirit. *Memory* was the source for John for his experiences with Jesus in history. *Direct experience* helped to shape and mold these memories to the present needs of the church. Finally, the *expectation* of the Second Coming and the ultimate consummation of all things projected John into God's eternal kingdom.

This dissection of time is necessary, but it falsifies reality. In a spiritual moment, these things happen *all at once*. This is what makes time such a difficult dimension. Contemporary physics has done us a great service in showing us that time is not a constant or an absolute. It is infinitely malleable. In the bending (but never breaking) of time, all kinds of things may and do happen. This is the source of miracles. This mystical insight does not disprove or invalidate the axoms and hypotheses of science. It does assert, however, the reality of other dimensions. The fourth dimension may, therefore, intimate other dimensions of which our philosophy and theology have as yet no grasp.

In any case, everything is transformed in time. Time is the dimension of transformation and transcendence. Because Jesus travels through pores in time, he can be present where he is needed: in memory, in direct experience, and in anticipation and expectation. He taught the great lesson to his disciples that time is indeed porous. Spiritually, sacramentally, and mystically, time can be transcended.

Jesus' most difficult task, like a cosmic Peter Pan, is to teach his disciples to fly between time and eternity, between this world and God's infinity. In his high priestly prayer, Jesus remembered and hoped:

And now I am no longer in the world, but they are in the world, and I am coming to you. . . . But now I am coming to you, and I speak these things in the world so that they may have my joy made complete in themselves. . . . As you have sent me into the world, so I have sent them into the world. And for their sakes I sanctify myself, so that they also may be sanctified in truth" (17:11, 13, 18-19).

Disciples of Jesus are to become time travelers even as he is a time traveler. Through their spiritual transcendence, perfectability, and sanctification, they are able to move back and forth between this "world" of darkness and evil to God's eternal kingdom of reality, light, life, truth, and glory. By connecting the two worlds through overcoming the limitations of time, they are able both to affirm and to continue Jesus' work of saving the world from itself.

The Fourth Gospel is filled with the disciples' difficulties in understanding what Jesus meant in his curious juxtaposition of time and eternity. In a famous passage, Jesus provided the disciples with the assurance that there was indeed a place for them beyond this world and a way to get there. Thomas replied with frustration, "Lord, we do not know where you are going. How can we know the way?" Jesus' response surely did little to help Thomas' confusion: "I am the way, and the truth, and the life. No one comes to the Father except through me" (14:6). The problem here is that Thomas and the others were still thinking in earthbound time and space. The "place" here probably should be translated into time categories. When Jesus said, "In my Father's house there are many dwelling places" (14:2), he is talking about eternal "dwelling." Heaven is more a "time" than a "place." It is the "place" of quality "time" and relationships.

For Jesus, in the Gospel of John, the key to heaven is the "glory" of God. *Glory* is Jesus' word for the quality of eternal life. At the climax of his ministry, as throughout his earthly life, Jesus kept his eyes on the glory of God. He said,

The hour has come for the Son of Man to be glorified. Very truly, I tell you, unless a grain of wheat falls into the earth and dies, it remains just a single grain; but if it dies, it bears much fruit. (12:23-24).

Likewise, Jesus called (and calls) his disciples to live for the glory of God. If they fail to do so, if they lose touch with the eternal, it is because they seek their own glory. Jesus commented on this as well: "How can you believe when you accept glory from one another and do not seek the glory that comes from the one who alone is God?" (5:44).

For John, this is the key to eternal life and to the meaning of resurrection as well. In Chapter 20, at the dramatic climax of his ministry, Jesus continued to manifest the glory of God to his disciples, and to call them to live in this way as well. Indeed, this is how Mary of Magdela and Thomas the Twin came to experience the glory of the risen Lord.

Early on Easter morning, Mary came to the tomb to complete the task of preparing the body for burial. When she did not find the body of Jesus, she asked a person she assumed to be the gardener where it had been taken (v. 15). Jesus then spoke her name, "Mary!" and history was forever changed.

Thomas, the doubting disciple, missed Jesus' first visit (v. 24). He declared that he would not believe what the others had seen unless he was able to touch the wounds in Jesus' hands and side. Only one week later, he had the opportunity to do this, but exclaimed instead, "My Lord and my God!" as Jesus appeared to the disciples gathered in the Upper Room.

Both Mary and Thomas transcended the bonds of space and time and witnessed the eternal glory of God through Jesus Christ. When Jesus asked Thomas, "Have you believed because you have seen me?" the answer was obviously "yes." The next statement was not a rebuke, but a blessing to disciples of spiritual sight: "Blessed are those who have not seen and yet have come to believe" (v. 29). In Thomas' case, it was true: "Seeing was believing." But spiritual seeing is infinitely superior to physical sight. John carried this emphasis all the way through to the benediction which closes the chapter: "But these [signs] are written so that you may come to believe that Jesus is the Messiah, the Son of God, and that through

believing you may have life in his name" (20:31). True disciples
come to sight and life spiritually as they understand themselves in
terms of God's eternity. Discipleship is living through time into
eternity.

The fourth dimension of discipleship is spiritual, sacramental,
and mystical. As important as the dimensions of height, depth, and
breadth are, they are only related to space. If one continues to view
discipleship spatially, one will lack transcendence. John's Gospel
adds the dimension of time and thereby opens the windows of
eternity. Without this dimension, discipleship could lose that eternal perspective, which is needed to sustain obedience, sacrifice, and
witness in the world and in time. With it, the other dimensions are
finally integrated and completed in a vision of what God is doing
through all of time.

PILOT TO COPILOT

In John's Gospel, Peter plays an interesting role in the development of the drama of glory. Several clues suggest that Peter had
real difficulty in learning how to live for God's glory, rather than
his own. Prior to Jesus' crucifixion and resurrection, for example,
Peter asked Jesus, "Where are you going?". Jesus explained that
Peter would not be able to follow now, but that later he would.
Then Peter, still thinking in literal and physical terms, asked,
"Lord, why can I not follow you now? I will lay down my life for
you" (13:37). Jesus then ironically tells him that, far from laying
down his life, Peter will soon deny him.

Likewise, there are indications of Peter's struggle in the beach
scene in Chapter 21. Here Peter and the others were fishing. The
risen Lord, standing on the shore, told them where to cast their
nets. When they obeyed him, they were scarcely able to handle the
harvest of fish. When they came on shore, they found that Jesus had
prepared a breakfast of fish and bread for them. (Clearly, for John,

this special last meal had eucharistic overtones.) After the sacramental meal, Jesus talked seriously with Peter.

He asked Peter, "Do you love me more than these?" (v. 15). Jesus' question probably referred to "these" fish. Peter had just become the most successful fisherman folks in that area had ever seen. The question might be translated, Is your love for Jesus able to transcend the glory of this world? Peter avowed his love for Jesus just as he had before the betrayal.

But then Jesus pursued the same question two more times. Each time, Peter answered in the affirmative—"Yes, Lord, you know I love you"—but Jesus responded as well, "Tend my sheep." Can you imagine how Peter felt when Jesus posed the question a third time? Surely the guilt of his three denials came down upon his shoulders as a nearly unbearable burden. I can imagine his responding in almost inaudible words, heavy with pain and remorse, "Lord, you know everything; you know that I love you" (v. 17). But Jesus still replied, "Feed my sheep."

In this curious dialogue, Peter the *fisherman* is asked symbolically to do the work of a *shepherd*. Is he really suited for this work? Can he leave the lake region, where he is so capable, and ascend to the highlands for a shepherd's lifestyle? Can he leave his little world and enter into another dimension of service? He glories in his work as a fisherman, but can he become a pastor who witnesses to the glory of God as manifested in Jesus Christ?

Peter's struggle to live for God's glory and, thus, to accept eternal life then confronts a final obstacle—his rivalry with John (vv. 20, 21). Peter did not realize that this rivalry was also a part of the "these" that Jesus asked him to give up. Peter continued to be worried about his own glory. Rather than opening himself to the glory of God in the presence of Christ, he turned, looked at John, and asked, "What about him?" (v. 21). Peter was still trying to evaluate his standing by comparing himself to others. Jesus' word to Peter was simple and direct, "Follow me."

In this beach scene, Jesus' actions again touch three modes of time simultaneously. He is present with God in his risen glory. He is present with Peter, with John, and with others on the beach, teaching his final earthly lessons about discipleship. He is also present to the church, urging an end to useless and divisive speculation. Church members, like Peter, are warned not to insist on their own glory, not to use the fellowship of the church for the business of gossip and rivalry. The spiritual dimension can be missed entirely if one is caught up in worldly concerns.

Jesus knew well the potential greatness of his friend, Peter. He also knew that Peter could not serve the church if he remained caught up in every wave of petty rivalry and speculation. He used the strongest words possible to strengthen the character of a man destined to be one of the greatest pastors in the history of the church. He directly applied the love commandment to Peter and connected it with the imperative of discipleship: "Follow me."

What was taking place on that beach was a changing of command, an expanding of Peter's horizon. Jesus was calling Peter to a new level of ministry to others. Peter had many natural gifts. He would not, however, fulfill them if he remained interested only in the glory of this world, or if he continued to evaluate himself in comparison with others.

The dialogue with Jesus was painful, but it was also realistic. Peter had to learn to keep before him the glory of the Lord. He had to develop a taste for eternity, to give up his competition with John, and to cease being intimidated by the penetrating insights of the other disciples. To sum this up in a vivid image, Peter had to come to a place in life where he could trust Jesus as the "pilot" of the church and see himself as the "copilot." It is not Peter, John, or anyone else who is ultimately in charge of the future, but Jesus himself, the church's eternal pilot.

Peter initially stumbled at the job description of the copilot. He was a plodding disciple who got sidetracked by matters of the world. Through the love of his Lord and of God's people, however, Peter came to the same high level of spirituality as his brother disciple

John. When he let go of the bulging nets and took up the shepherd's staff, he was able to see spiritually, sacramentally, and mystically. These were at first the gifts farthest from his nature. Through the love and nurture of his Lord, however, Peter grew to spiritual insight and to new life. As a pastor, Peter learned to fly with his Lord, ever copilot with Jesus securely guiding the flight of the church into eternity. He came to understand and to accept Jesus' prayer for him and for all disciples: "Father, I desire that those also, whom you have given me, may be with me where I am, to see my glory, which you have given me because you loved me before the foundation of the world" (17:24).

QUESTIONS FOR STUDY AND DISCUSSION

1. We sometimes hear of experiences in which the presence of something beautiful, awe-inspiring, or terribly frightening, seems to make time stand still. We speak of memories so vivid that the past seems to live again. We may look forward to something with such great anticipation and joy that it would be true to say that much of our happiness takes place before the "thing itself" actually arrives. Have you had experiences similar to these? If so, describe one or two.

2. Human life is best described as a "quality of life in time." What do experiences like those you described above tell you about our human capacity to transcend time? To live in different "modes" of time?

3. Have you ever thought of eternal life as a *quality* of life beginning in time for those who believe? How does this concept from John's Gospel challenge or confirm your ideas about eternal life?

4. Think about how Jesus taught that loving others and living for God's glory rather than for our own is part of a quality of life that is eternal. Can you think of anyone you have known personally whose life seems to prove the truth of Jesus' teachings? Jot down your thoughts.

5. Which matters in your daily life (or in the life of your congregation) might take on a different aspect if you were able to see them more clearly in the light of eternity? Explain.

6. The sacrament of Holy Communion is an experience that transcends time. In light of all you have learned in this chapter, write down your thoughts in response to this statement.

6

Discipleship for a New Age

THE NTH DEGREE

We have explored the dimensions of height, depth, breadth, and time in the four Gospels. It would be nice to be able to say that we had somehow "cubed" the Gospels, but cubing is only the third power. No word in physical science deals with the fourth degree. Mathematics is much better suited than physics for dealing with discipleship because it has the ability to consider infinity. In mathematics, any power beyond the third is simply referred to as "the nth degree." This is useful here because it is open-ended. We have studied discipleship to the nth degree. This means we have carefully investigated four dimensions of discipleship, but we also acknowledge the possibility of more dimensions in the life of the contemporary believer. This does not mean that we can exceed the scope and power of Jesus or of the New Testament. It does mean, however, that the disciple of Jesus Christ is expected to continue to do his work, and even to do greater things. Jesus said to his first disciples,

> Very truly, I tell you, the one who believes in me will also do the works that I do and, in fact, will do greater works than these, because I am going to the Father. I will do whatever you ask in my name, so that the Father may be glorified in the Son. If in my name you ask me for anything, I will do it (John 14:12-14).

This "greater" is discipleship to the nth degree. The first disciples were offered the ability to respond and to follow the Master in the four dimensions described by the Gospels. They were not limited, however, to these four. The contemporary disciple has an even greater opportunity, for the words of Jesus suggest progressively greater works in his name. Before discussing what this might mean, let us summarize what we have learned about discipleship from our study of the Gospels.

A disciple of Jesus Christ, according to Matthew, is one who looks up to the Master, hearing and obeying creatively his teachings and following him wherever he goes. This disciple places such profound trust in God and in God's Son, that he or she is able to be free from everyday cares, being present, in the highest sense, to him or herself. The disciple is one who is responsible to the Lord. This person is able both to carry out assigned tasks in accordance with the talents provided by God, and to hold others responsible in a reasonable manner. This disciple is able to accept authority from Jesus and to carry out Jesus' work in the world. In doing these things, the disciple comes to resemble the Lord whom he or she serves.

The disciple of Jesus Christ, according to Mark, has to face suffering, sacrifice, and even death in the same way that Jesus did. The life of martyrdom is not one which the disciple seeks, but it is also not one which can be entirely avoided either. The Servant of God is destined to suffer in order to change the situation of humanity. This redemptive suffering at the hands of the powers of this world opens the believer to the reality of God's kingdom in human history. The disciple must learn to distinguish appearance from reality by having eyes opened to the war that is going on all around. Jesus engaged in conflict with the powers of evil, sin, and death. At the cross, he lost the battle, but won the war. The victory of the Son of God was accomplished only through his suffering and death. There is enough here to frighten any disciple to death! Faith in Jesus, however, conquers this fear and allows the disciple to take heart and stand up to the pain and suffering implicit in the life and death of discipleship.

According to Luke, Jesus Christ is the universal Savior of humanity. He saves the disciple from narrowness, bigotry, pettiness, and exclusivity. Being a disciple means having the same passion for love and justice the Master has. This means going out of one's way to serve and to save the poor, the ill, the hungry, and the utterly wretched person, who has otherwise no champion or defender. It means seeing the big picture and not getting caught up in details. It also means, however, being methodical, especially in terms of going out into the world to spread the gospel to every human being in every nation. Being a responsible disciple means being a missionary for Christ. The disciple knows that he or she will be held accountable and eagerly expects to give account. This person observes carefully and bears witness in inspired testimony to God's grace in life. The disciple is one who knows personally that life has been turned around by the work of the Holy Spirit. Through the continued work of the Spirit, the disciple is emboldened for witness again and again. This conversion experience through the Spirit changes all values and standards for the believer.

Finally, according to John, the disciple is one who learns the difference between time and eternity. This means seeing everything from God's perspective. Time, which seems absolute to the earthbound, appears relative from the perspective of eternity. When one sees Jesus as a time traveler, it becomes clear that he can be present in more than one dimension at any time. This makes way for the real presence of the Lord in the life of the disciple and in the worship of the church. The one who is present is the one sent from God. Jesus is the divine creative wisdom through whom God has made everything. To understand him is to read the very mind of God. The disciple is one who has already entered upon the way of eternal life, one "born from above," one who is able to love God, self, and the other person with the same love that God has for all of creation. Jesus is the very incarnation of this self-sacrificial love. He both exemplifies it and commands the disciple to enact it. This command would be impossible without the support of the Spirit-Advocate. To the disciple, the Holy Spirit is the Presence of God with us for sustaining, supporting, and counseling constancy. For the disciple, time is porous, just as it is for the Lord. This means that Jesus is really present in memory, direct experience, and expectation. The fullness of the spiritual moment enables the disciple to transcend the world of darkness and to participate in the glory of the Lord. This is a resurrection faith that has already left death behind.

SIMON PETER, THE DISCIPLE FOR ALL SEASONS

Before arriving at some conclusions about what discipleship should be in the contemporary situation, we need to summarize our study of the role of Peter as "everyman" in the Gospels. His growth as a disciple provides the most vivid example in the New Testament of a life transformed.

Simon Peter probably heard enough puns on his colorful name, "Rock," to last a lifetime! Looking back on his life, he very likely was amazed at how he grew to fit the name. This man, who was so uncertain of his faith and of himself, became for his Teacher the foundation and the primary authority for the church. He learned to look up to Jesus as the source of his ministry. The church came to look up to him in the same way.

Peter gave the appearance of being a person who had everything figured out. He seemed to be confident and in control. His daring and strength were already proverbial before Jesus called him into his disciple band. Not even Peter knew how much this was a desperate bluff, designed to hide his own cowardice. His denial of his Lord took away the mask. He felt completely disgraced and worthless. The risen Lord, however, forgave him and healed him of his fear. He has become for the church one of its greatest martyrs and saints, whose courage is legendary.

As much as Peter tried to understand Jesus' teachings about justice and deeds of love, he still was a child of prejudice and bigotry. Surely God did not intend for him to abandon the exclusive customs of an observant Jew in the first century. It was all right for Jesus to associate with Samaritans, Gentiles, sinners, and ritually impure people, but Peter didn't want to be asked to do such things.

In his career as apostle, however, after the death and resurrection of Jesus, Peter became a major force in mediating the discussion between the different Christian communities. Tolerance, openness, and a broad vision of the church were difficult for him. He came to stand, however, side by side with Paul—who had so long been his rival—as one of the greatest exponents of the Gentile mission, and of missionary theology in general.

Although Peter was certainly not the most worldly of the disciples, it is still true that he may well have been one of the least spiritual. He is certainly the most literal. He simply got lost when Jesus went off into some spiritual ecstasy. He resented John's intuitive grasp of Jesus' message about eternal life. He saw much more clearly the administrative function of Jesus' ministry than the sacramental and mystical levels. He found the intensity of Jesus' elevated speech oppressive and almost incomprehensible. Each time Peter thought he had caught up with Jesus' dazzling spiritual presence, he found that the Lord had transcended his understanding and gotten ahead of him again. This came to its climax in the Upper Room, when the risen Lord appeared to him and to the others. Peter learned that he had to share with John the ministerial leadership of the young church. This ministry was both practical and spiritual. Being the great pastor of the church meant he had to administer *and* minister. This fisherman learned to be one of the greatest shepherds in the history of the church.

THE ESSENTIAL FOURNESS

The number "four" is important in the history of the church. In the Bible, it generally stands for the earth with its four corners. Combined with the number "three," which usually represents heaven, it forms the perfect number "seven," the number of fullness, completion, and infinity. Wesleyan theology speaks of a "quadrilateral," which includes scripture, tradition, reason, and experience. This broad, tolerant, and balanced approach has been quite successful. The contemporary philosopher, Martin Heidegger, spoke of a basic "fourfold" nature of reality, which consists of "earth and sky, divinities and mortals."[21] There is an essential "four-coordinate system, space-time."[22] We have studied in the four Gospels a fundamental fourness.

There can be no "gospel harmony" here. The very idea of "harmonizing" the Gospels is an offense, when one thinks of the integrity of each dimension. Remember the illustration of the "knothole gangs" at baseball games (page 4 above)? Now hear another parable. The story is told of a man who invited a friend to go with him to a baseball game. He was intrigued by the fact that his friend brought along a board with a hole in the center. The man asked his friend why he brought the board. The friend replied that he had never learned to watch the entire game at once. He learned as a boy to have a perspective on the game according to the particular knothole in front of him. In the same way, we must learn to respect the particular perspective and integrity of each Gospel. We also need to recognize however, that the wholeness of the gospel is greater than any one of its parts.

There must remain four Gospels and four dimensions of discipleship. This cannot be changed or compromised. Heidegger made the following rhapsodic statement about his understanding of the "fourfold": "By a *primal* oneness the four—earth and sky, divinities and mortals—belong together in one."[23] It is precisely "the *primal* oneness" of the gospel which necessitates the fourfold presentation of discipleship. The three dimensions of space (height, depth, and breadth) and the dimension of time are all necessary and cannot be abandoned. They provide the "coordinates" that we must have to live in space and time. To multiply the first three together would give us the undistinguished cubic volume of space. Multiplication with the addition of the fourth dimension does not exist, of course. We could imagine it, however, as a quantum designation of the volume of discipleship.

Let us further imagine that we could take this abstract quantification of discipleship and turn it into multiple bytes for church computers. Bureaucratic minds in church headquarters would be abuzz with ideas. Their work would have a sophistication never before possible. A kind of quantum theory of discipleship would be possible in which the energy of genuine followers of Jesus Christ could be scientifically identified, specified, and measured in definite units called *quanta*. This entity could then be used to design and develop an equation by which experts in discipleship could predict with almost absolute certainty the discipleship coefficients of all Christians. That equation could be represented in a formula such as this one: $CD = \dfrac{H \times D \times B}{T^2}$. Christian Discipleship = Height $\times$ Depth $\times$ Breadth over Time squared. Program planners and church growth experts would be able to carry out their work without hesitation. The science of discipleship would be established.

Thank goodness this is only a disciple's nightmare! Discipleship cannot be quantified. It can be measured only in quality terms. The essential fourness of the Gospels cannot be cooked or blended together to form some sort of generic discipleship mass. There is no single whole to it. The four Gospels do, however, present a holistic vision of discipleship in which the dimensions complement each other in the same way as do the dimensions of reality in time and space. Indeed, that is what discipleship for the Christian is: living the Christian faith in responsible obedience to the discipline of the Master.

DIVERSITY AND DISCIPLES

Discipleship will remain multidimensional and polychromatic as it was for the first followers of Jesus. The variety is as mathematically infinite as the number of individuals who choose to become disciples of Jesus Christ. It is as inexhaustible as the number of shades of color in a rainbow. Discipleship cannot be reduced to a formula or an orthodoxy. It involves the actualization of a human potential so vast as to dwarf our means and methods of computation. Jesus, as the Grand Master of creation, saw into the lives of his first disciples and drew out a part—a significant part, but only a part—of the vast potential. So it is with disciple-making today. Discipleship can never become a science. It must remain a strange and wonderful art, a creative miracle.

We in the church must be involved in the process of discipleship. This involves introducing prospective disciples to the Master. No relationship is possible without the introduction. We who think that we know Jesus, but are afraid to share him, clearly do not know Jesus.

Once the relationship is begun, we can nurture and support the potential disciple. That is what the church should be about. This care and feeding cannot happen, however, in situations where high-pressure power, career, and ego games are going on. Everything in the church should center around the simplicity and profundity of the relationship of the disciple with the Master. Anything that detracts from that is of the evil one, and not of God. Disciples grow in an open, tolerant, catholic environment. The four Gospels could be said to present four different authentic positions. Each one gives us a valid picture of Jesus and how to relate to him. Each one presents a genuine process for discipleship. Jesus is the universal Master, however, to whom all disciples come, no matter from what direction they are coming. When one perspective is selected as "the best" and held over against other equally valid ones, discipleship suffers and the gospel is falsified.

Multidimensional and polychromatic discipleship must have the greatest diversity not only at the source, but also at the destination. When one actually observes a rainbow, one sees that the colors extend in bands over a giant bridge without ever crossing, mixing, or altering the width of each band. Each of us has a proper point of departure within our faith stance, and each of us has a connecting point with the Master. There need be no rivalry among us and no jealousy for the attention of the Master.

The results of discipleship training can be reflected in vastly different lifestyles. Diversity was written all over the original disciple band. There was creative disagreement between different individuals and interpretations also. The relationships between Peter and Paul, and Peter and John provide good examples. There is no phony harmony here or saccharine solution. Disciples disagree, but they do so in the full assurance that no one "possesses" Christ. Each disciple has a different perspective, a different mission, and, therefore, different priorities. There are many occasions for both/and—not just for either/or. In any case, the source is the same: Jesus Christ. And the goal is the same: the kingdom. Diversity between these two fixed points is permissible, so long as the words and actions used do not falsify either the source or the goal.

DISCIPLESHIP IN A POSTMODERN ERA

Our time has been described as a "postmodern" era. It is a bit difficult to decide what this might mean. It does indicate the passing of the idea of "modernity." It may be the case that modernity never arrived. There are naturally some broken expectations, as well as some renewed anticipations, of whatever it is that will come next. T. S. Eliot spoke of a feeling in our time that something has died and that something is struggling to be born. We are not sure, however, what it is that has died or what it is that is about to be born. Mark C. Taylor has expressed this in a kind of riddle of postmodernity:

Postmodern awareness is born of the recognition that the past that was never present eternally returns as the future that never arrives to displace all contemporaneity and defer forever the presence of the modern. [24]

This quote reflects a profound temporal disturbance, not unlike Augustine's statement that he had been "torn between the times." Taylor quotes the French philosopher, Maurice Blanchot, in a statement that indicates the modern predicament:

> In time's absence what is new renews nothing; what is present is not contemporary; what is present presents nothing, but represents itself and belongs henceforth and always to return.[25]

As bleak as this diagnosis of the malady of modernity is, however, it can be understood as a preparation for the gospel.

The Gospel which speaks most immediately to our postmodern predicament is John. The discovery of the fourth dimension offers an entrance to this Gospel and to the New Testament as a whole. Our greatest need is spiritual. Our greatest problem is a difficulty in time. In overcoming the deceptions of the modern period, we are open to something new, to the Novum, the truly innovative. We are frozen between the times, however, like the curious characters in "Waiting for Godot." We cannot return to the past, but do not know how to enter the present. In other words, we are in the situation of the first disciples before Jesus of Nazareth came along and called them. We are like a teenager the week before the prom, sitting beside the telephone: We are profoundly potentially callable!

Too often in the church, we do not really think we have much to say. All of our actions betray that fact. It may be the case, however, that an unsettled society is out there, similar to our teenager, just waiting to be called. However, not just any call will do. People today are hungry for spirituality. This is especially true of Christians. Perhaps the greatest Roman Catholic theologian of our century, Karl Rahner, has said: "The Christian of tomorrow will be a mystic, one who has experienced something, or he will be nothing."[26] This is an extremely telling statement for discipleship and for spirituality.

One of the things we should learn from all of the disappointing experiments of the modern age is that there really is "nothing new under the sun." Discipleship is today what it was for the first disciples: An obedient follower of Jesus Christ accepts suffering, is willing to consider everyone as neighbor, is prepared to struggle for love and justice, and has a passion for eternity which begins in this life or never. The content does not and cannot change without falsification, duplicity, and deceit. "Prepackaged, instant discipleship" was served up by the indulgence hawkers of Luther's day and is a major product of the so-called "electronic church" today. It will not work.

The major change for a postmodern era might be a reversal of order. Christians have always read the Bible backwards anyway. Everything begins for the disciple with Easter. We really pretend we do not know the conclusion when we read the Bible. John Calvin said that we should read the entire Bible "with Christological spectacles." Because of the unique discovery of the dimension of time and its relativity, the spirituality of John's Gospel is not hidden for us in the same way that it has been for many previous centuries. For the postmodern Christian, the redemption of time can then logically and theologically lead to the redemption of space, represented in breadth, depth, and height. This would begin our study all over again, but this time necessarily under the controlling theme of spirituality. This task must be left to the disciplined time traveler, the disciple who lives within and yet transcends the bonds of modernity and contemporaneity with the risen Lord. This requires rewriting Blanchot's tragic riddle of postmodern existence: "In eternity's presence, what is new renews everything; what is present is in the highest sense contemporary, representing the Lord, and belonging henceforth and always to transcendence." In the face of "postmodern blues," contemporary discipleship must assert the good news that in Jesus Christ, God has redeemed time and space in all of their dimensions!

QUESTIONS FOR STUDY AND DISCUSSION

1. What does it mean that discipleship is open-ended? How would you distinguish the open-endedness of discipleship from mere indifference?

2. Having completed this study, which of the dimensions would you say is most like your own experience of discipleship today? Which is least like your experience?

3. Can you see different dimensions of discipleship at work in your congregation? Identify some of these differences.

4. Would you say that the diversity of discipleship in your life and/or in your congregation is a sign of strength in following Jesus, or weakness? Explain.

5. The malady of our culture in the postmodern era is to be, like Augustine, "torn between the times," waiting for life in the present without fruitful memory of the past or meaningful hope for the future. How might the witness of John's Gospel to Jesus, the time traveler, help us in dealing with and addressing this malady?

6. What dimension(s) of discipleship most capture(s) your imagination and call(s) for your attention at this time? Write a brief prayer/letter to Jesus expressing your hope to remember and follow him.

Endnotes

1. William Barclay, *The Gospel of Matthew,* Vol. 1 (Philadelphia: The Westminster Press, 1975), p. 255.

2. Ibid., p. 258.

3. St. Augustine, *The Confessions* (Philadelphia: The Westminster Press, 1955), p. 268.

4. Søren Kierkegaard, *Christian Discourses* (London: Oxford University Press, 1939), p. 77.

5. Dietrich Bonhoeffer, *The Cost of Discipleship* (New York: Macmillan, 1949), p. 77.

6. Nathaniel Hawthorne, "The Great Stone Face," *Hawthorne's Short Stories,* ed. Newton Arvin (New York: Alfred A. Knopf, 1954), pp. 374-75.

7. Lamar Williamson, Jr., *Interpretation: Mark* (Atlanta: John Knox Press, 1983), p. 16.

8. Søren Kierkegaard, *Stages on Life's Way* (New York: Shocken Books, 1967), pp. 430ff.

9. Bonhoeffer, p. 47.

10. Ibid., p. 102.

11. William Barclay, *The Gospel of Mark* (Philadelphia: The Westminster Press, 1975), p. 321.

12. David Lowes Watson, *Covenant Discipleship Congregational Guide* (Nashville: Discipleship Resources, 1985), p. 5.

13. David Lowes Watson, *Accountable Discipleship* (Nashville: Discipleship Resources, 1986), p. 15.

14. *The Treasury of Religious Verse,* Compiled by Donald T. Kauffmann (Westwood, N.J.: Fleming H. Revell Co., 1962), p. 8. Reproduced by permission of the *New York Herald Tribune.*

15. John Boslough and Bruce Dale, "The Enigma of Time," *National Geographic,* Vol. 177, No. 3, March 1990, p. 111.

16. Ibid., p. 118.

17. William Barclay, *The Gospel of John,* Vol. 1 (Philadelphia: The Westminster Press, 1975), p. 10.

18. Ibid., p. 36.

19. William Barclay, *The Gospel of John,* Vol. 2 (Philadelphia: The Westminster Press, 1975), pp. 207-08.

20. Augustine, *Confessions,* p. 259.

21. Martin Heidegger, *Basic Writings* (New York: Harper and Row, 1977), pp. 327-28.

22. Boslough and Dale, "The Enigma of Time," p. 118.

23. Heidegger, p. 327.

24. *Deconstruction in Context,* ed. Mark C. Taylor (Chicago: The University of Chicago Press, 1986), p. 36.

25. Ibid.

26. Quoted in Ignacio Larrañaga, *Sensing Your Hidden Presence: Toward Intimacy with God* (Garden City, NY: Image Books, 1987), p. 11.

For Further Reading

On the subject of Christian discipleship, one could scarcely find richer sources than the works of Søren Kierkegaard and Dietrich Bonhoeffer which are mentioned in the Endnotes (page 89). David Lowes Watson's exciting work on Covenant Discipleship is also cited in the text. There are a number of excellent orientations to the New Testament any serious student of the Bible would find interesting. These include:

Robert A. Spivey and D. Moody Smith, *Anatomy of the New Testament* (New York: Macmillan, 1989).

Howard Clark Kee, *Understanding the New Testament* (Englewood Cliffs, N.J.: Prentice-Hall, 1983).

John Drane, *Introducing the New Testament* (San Francisco: Harper and Row, 1986).

John Carmody, Denise Lardner Carmody and Gregory A. Robbins, *Exploring the New Testament* (Englewood Cliffs, N.J., 1986).

Commentaries are extremely valuable. *The Interpreters Bible* remains the standard for many readers. William Barclay's little volumes, published in *The Daily Study Bible Series* by Westminster Press, are extremely rich and profitable for the general student. More technical treatments are presented in the *Interpretation* series, published by Westminster/John Knox Publishers, and in *The Anchor Bible* commentaries, published by Doubleday.

The following titles are available from Discipleship Resources, P. O. Box 189, Nashville, TN 37202; (615) 340-7284.

THE MEANING OF THE WARMED HEART

Thirteen New Testament studies of biblical and modern disciples, by Donald English. Includes perceptive discussion questions. (Discipleship Resources, order no. DR050B)

WINDOWS ON THE PASSION

Donald English explores the meaning of Jesus' death through this lay Bible study of the Gospels. Includes brief prayers, scripture passages for reflection, and questions for discussion. (Discipleship Resources, order no. DR066B)

PORTRAITS OF CHRIST IN SCRIPTURE, Vol. 1

Robert W. Wingard presents a short-term group study of three images of Jesus, painted by the Gospels of Mark and John, and in the Letters of Paul. (Discipleship Resources, order no. DR047B)

THE WAY OF THE CROSS

A six-week study of the way of the cross, the way of redemptive suffering, by Joel B. Green. Includes questions for reflection/discussion. (Discipleship Resources, order no. DR103B)

LIFE BEGINS AT CHRIST

Alan Walker interprets the conversion experiences of six persons in the New Testament with the aim of understanding what transformed their lives. (Discipleship Resources, order no. EV095B)

JESUS CHRIST FOR TODAY

Study of the person and character of Jesus Christ in the Gospel of
Luke, by William Barclay. (Discipleship Resources, order no.
DR015B)